D0371656

WORLD

TURNED UPSIDE DOWN

Related Potomac Books Titles

Counterspy: Memoirs of a Counterintelligence Officer
in World War II and the Cold War
Richard Cutler

Special Agent, Vietnam: A Naval Intelligence Memoir
Douglass H. Hubbard

WORLD

TURNED UPSIDE DOWN

U.S. NAVAL INTELLIGENCE AND THE
EARLY COLD WAR STRUGGLE FOR GERMANY

Marvin B. Durning

Foreword by Robert K. Massie,
Pulitzer Prize–winning historian and biographer

Potomac Books, Inc.
Washington, D.C.

Library of Congress Cataloging-in-Publication Data
Durning, Marvin B., 1929–
  World turned upside down : U.S. naval intelligence and the early
Cold War struggle for Germany / Marvin B. Durning ; foreword by
Robert K. Massie.
    p. cm.
  Includes bibliographical references and index.
  ISBN 978-1-59797-134-8 (hbk. : alk. paper)
1. Durning, Marvin B., 1929– 2. Intelligence officers—United States—
Biography. 3. Military intelligence—United States—History—20th
century. 4. Military intelligence—Germany (West)—History—20th cen-
tury. 5. United States. Office of Naval Intelligence—History—20th cen-
tury. 6. Organisation Gehlen. 7. Cold War. I. Title. II. Title: U.S. naval
intelligence and the early cold war struggle for Germany.
  UB271.U52D87 2007
  359.3′432092—dc22
  [B]

                                                        2007025803

Printed in the United States of America on acid-free paper that meets
the American National Standards Institute Z39-48 Standard.

Potomac Books, Inc.
22841 Quicksilver Drive
Dulles, Virginia 20166

First Edition

10 9 8 7 6 5 4 3 2 1

To Val Rychly, the Skipper,
and to Jean

North
Sea

*Baltic
Sea*

NETH.

Amsterdam

Liège

BELG.

FRANCE

Kiel

Lübeck
Hamburg

Wilhelms-
haven   Bremerhaven
           Lüneburg
Bremen

Weser   Hannover   Aller

Braunschweig

WEST

Dortmund

Düsseldorf

Köln

Bonn

Fulda

Frankfurt

Mainz

Moselle

Main

Würzburg

Mannheim

Heidelberg

GERMANY

Strasbourg

Rhine

Stuttgart

Freiburg

Danube

Zürich

Bern

Rhine

SWITZ.

Rhine

Geneva

Grenoble

Ticino

Torino

Po

Rostock

Stettin

EAST

POLAND

Neisse

Berlin

Potsdam

Magdeburg

Elbe

Leipzig

GERMANY

Prague

Pilsen

CZECH.

Nuremburg

Augsburg

Linz

Danube

Munich

Inn

Salzburg

AUSTRIA

Innsbruck

Ljubljana

Trieste

Milan

ITALY

Venice

Po

Genoa

*Adriatic
Sea*

Ravenna

GERMANY
in the
Cold War

0   25   50   75   100
Miles

Karamales 2007

CONTENTS

FOREWORD

In March 1953, in brilliant sunshine and with a cold wind blowing off Narragansett Bay, Marvin Durning graduated from Officer Candidate School in Newport, Rhode Island, and for the first time put on the blue uniform with a single gold stripe on each sleeve that proclaimed him a brand new ensign in the U.S. Navy. Durning's route to Newport was special enough to mark him out from most of the young men who also became new ensigns that day. He was born and raised in New Orleans, his father was a U.S. Marine Corps officer who was killed before World War II, he went to Dartmouth and graduated summa cum laude, and he spent two years at Oxford on a Rhodes scholarship.

The Korean War was being fought while Durning was at Newport, and on graduating many of the neophyte ensigns left immediately for sea duty with the fleet, becoming junior watch-standers on the destroyers, cruisers, aircraft carriers, and logistic support ships that made up the task forces and task groups of the Navy around the world. Nevertheless, it was clear even then that the Korean War, a three-year struggle to hold on to a far-off peninsula in the northern Pacific, was only a fragment, a subdivision, of a far greater struggle that would loom over the world for most of the rest of the century. We know this struggle as the Cold War. Here, our primary adversary, the formidable conglomerate of military power and ideological aggression, was the Soviet Union. The Kremlin—with its hundreds (later thousands) of nuclear weapons, masses of aircraft, tanks, and soldiers in Central Europe, and its iron control of satellite nations on almost every continent—posed the ultimate threat. And in this context Marvin Durning was chosen to become involved in the greater world struggle. This involvement, which he describes in this fascinating book, took place in what, for a naval officer, was an unusual place.

After assignments at the Office of Naval Intelligence and aboard a destroyer, Durning was sent to a naval intelligence office in Munich, Germany, hundreds of miles from salt water. He was there in 1955 and participated in the final stages of the transformation of a defeated Germany into a respected democracy that gained full sovereignty, joining NATO, and beginning to rearm. At that time, Munich, like Berlin, was a nerve center of the Cold War, crowded with American soldiers, with German and Slav refugees, the home of Radio Liberty and Radio Free Europe, broadcasting to the Soviet Union and its satellites. In addition, Durning writes, the city "was a jungle of competing secret intelligence organizations: British, French, American, Russian, West and East German, Czech, Polish, and others." Beneath the calm surface of everyday life in Munich were agents and double agents, defections and interrogations that ended in death, kidnappings, and assassinations by bomb explosions and by poison dart pistols.

Under his remarkable commanding officer, CDR Vladimir Rychly, Durning served as de facto second in command of a small office of German intelligence specialists, which kept track of and dealt with items of normal naval interest: East bloc naval activities in the North Sea, the Baltic, the White Sea, and on the Danube River; the status of East German, Polish, and Soviet ports and naval bases; photos of warships, ship construction, fortifications, cargo-handling facilities, and dry docks. But in addition the office did much more. Under the direction of CDR Rychly, Soviet bloc defectors and border crossers from East Germany, some with information of naval interest, were interrogated. Known only to Rychly and Durning, former admirals of the World War II German navy, two of whom went on to become commanders of the navy of the Federal Republic of Germany, came often to secret meetings with Rychly, during which they worked together to plan and create a future West German navy.

Of equal interest are Durning's chapters on his relationship with the Gehlen Organization, the super-secret German intelligence and espionage organization that was sponsored and financed first by the U.S. Army, then by the Central Intelligence Agency. The organization was led by Gen. Reinhard Gehlen, formerly the German General Staff's chief of intelligence on the Soviet Union, especially its armed forces. After the German surrender, Gehlen and the U.S. Army reached agreement to cooperate. Gehlen recruited some of the best of his wartime staff, recovered his hidden intelligence files, and set to work for the benefit of the United States and a future democratic Germany. By 1955, the Gehlen organization, housed in a walled compound in the village of Pullach near Munich, employed several thousand people to collect and evaluate strategic and tactical intelligence from the Soviet bloc.

Durning's connection with this group began in his first days in Munich, when he became the U.S. Navy liaison officer to the Gehlen Organization's Navy Evaluation Section. Soon thereafter, he drove CDR Rychly and a man introduced as "Doktor Schneider" to an American air base where they boarded a Navy plane for a secret trip to the U.S. Sixth Fleet in the Mediterranean. Later Durning learned that "Doktor Schneider" was Gen. Reinhard Gehlen himself. Durning made weekly visits to the Gehlen Organization and, when necessary, practiced such tradecraft as blandly dropping a package into the supermarket shopping cart of a female CIA operative.

It was not the Gehlen Organization, however, that plunged Durning into sudden and deep involvement in derailing a Soviet effort to kill West German Chancellor Konrad Adenauer by beaming high-intensity radiation at the elderly statesman as he slept during his visit to Moscow in September 1955. Durning, alone at the Munich station when the information about the assassination attempt was received, sent coded Top-Secret messages to Washington; the alarm was spread. Adenauer slept somewhere else and survived.

Some of Durning's descriptions—of the atmosphere of a crowded Munich beer hall, of driving on "a wet two lane asphalt road, passing snow covered fields, under the heavy grey clouds of a north European winter"—resemble pages from John Le Carré's novels. Other pages—describing the personal life of a young American surrounded by the shadowy figures of older men, former adversaries, former admirals, a veteran U-boat commander, survivors of the savage, merciless fighting on the Eastern Front—make plain how far this young officer had come from home. So, also, does his account of the life and behavior of a young, attractive, and despairing German woman who viewed him as a passport to a better life.

One last thing: I knew Marvin Durning at Oxford; I graduated from Newport OCS with him in the same class; I have seen him, off and on, for fifty-five years. And yet, everything he has written, I learned for the first time when I read this book.

Robert K. Massie
Irvington, New York

AUTHOR'S NOTE

This account of the dramatic events in the early Cold War struggle over the future of Germany, hence of Europe, and the important role U.S. Naval Intelligence played in that struggle is based on my personal experience as a naval intelligence officer assigned to duty at the Navy's secret office in Munich.

Names and cover names are correct as they were in 1955–56, except for a few people for whom I have invented names either to avoid any possible harm or embarrassment to them or their families or simply because I never knew or have forgotten their real names. In each case where an invented name is used it is identified as such in the text at the invention's first appearance.

The facts I state are accurate to the best of my knowledge, information, and belief. My experience in Germany was intense and my memory of those days in Germany is keen. I have written much in dialogue form because dialogue provided me a means more accurate than straight narrative to portray the reality of the situation. Naturally I don't recall every word that was said over fifty years ago, but the essence of each dialogue is correct. Similarly, at the beginning of chapter 3 I have described what ran through Val Rychly's mind as he started his day. I can do so because I now know his situation at the time and his morning routine. Years later he told me his thoughts on the day of my arrival.

ACKNOWLEDGMENTS

First things first: my thanks are due to my wife Jean, who gently but persistently encouraged me to write this book, helped in every phase of my work—research, editing, typing, and critiquing the book—and kept my spirits up as the months passed and the end seemed to retreat before me.

I give my most heartfelt thanks to Robert K. Massie, a Pulitzer Prize winner, who volunteered to write the foreword to this book. He is a friend indeed.

I am grateful to Waldtraut Parnitzki, the widow of Max Parnitzki, their daughter Marion, and Marion's husband Petr Doubrava, who have all given many hours to this effort, finding and reviewing Max's papers, providing photos, discussing his history in detail with me. Petr drove us around Munich and its environs in 2004 so that we could revisit the places prominent in the story, including both the mansion at Possart Platz 3, which housed our intelligence office, and the compound containing the headquarters of the Gehlen Organization in Pullach. Waldtraut and Marion read an early version of the book and made valuable comments.

I am grateful to Hannelore Rychly, widow of Vladimir Rychly, for hospitality extended to me and to Jean many times over the years and for the documents and recollections of facts she has provided. Hannelore allowed me to copy Val Rychly's travel diary for 1945–48, his MI-6 and naval attaché years. She gave me a photo of Val with General Heusinger and other American and German officers aboard a U.S. aircraft carrier and a photo of a happy reunion of James Critchfield and his wife Lois with General Gehlen's family at the Rychlys' home in Neu Grünwald.

My genuine thanks also to friends in Seattle: Darlene Cox, formerly my legal secretary, gave me forceful pushes at various times. H. Robert Widditsch, who lived a number of years in Germany and is familiar with life there; Charles Ehlert, a lawyer who is also a knowledgeable student of history; and Mike Layton, paratrooper, journalist, and author—all read an early draft of the book and gave me useful reactions. I give special thanks to Ann Widditsch for help with this book and for help many times in the past.

My gratitude goes to Lois Critchfield, James Critchfield's widow, for her interest and comments and for providing some relevant photos; to Jeffrey G. Barlow, Ph.D., historian at the U.S. Naval Historical Center, Washington, D.C.; and to Dr. Douglas C. Peifer, historian at the U.S. Air Force Air War College, Maxwell Air Force Base, for their insightful and encouraging comments.

Finally, thanks are due to my team of editors at Potomac Books: Rick Russell, Don Jacobs, Julie Kimmel, Marla Traweek, Katie Freeman, John Church, and Claire Noble. Each contributed to the metamorphosis of my manuscript to this book.

I alone am responsible for any errors in this book.

PROLOGUE

There is a story about the surrender of the British troops under Lord Cornwallis to the American general George Washington at Yorktown, Virginia, in 1781. This surrender ended the fighting in the American Revolution, made possible a new and independent nation in North America, and upset the relative power positions of the nations of Europe and their colonial empires around the world.

In 1781 Great Britain was the richest and most powerful nation in the Western world. Yet, after six years of fighting, Britain had to admit defeat by the rag-tag amateur army and militias of its rebellious American colonies, fighting a guerilla war, assisted by aid from Britain's European rivals, France and Holland. The resulting American victory was entirely unexpected, and it is said that the surrendering British soldiers marched off the battlefield to the beat of their military band playing an English ballad first published in 1643, "The World Turned Upside Down."

Other examples of unexpected rapid and fundamental change appear from time to time in history. One of these is the transformation of defeated Germany from an aggressive totalitarian Nazi dictatorship and mortal enemy of the United States, Britain, and France to a respected democracy and ally of the Western powers in the defense of Europe against the armies of the Soviet Union and its allies. All this happened in little more than ten years following Germany's unconditional surrender on May 8, 1945, and it changed the course of history in Europe, North America, and the wider world.

The Largest Single Event in Human History

The Second World War is the largest single event in human history, fought across six of the world's seven continents and all its oceans. It

1

killed fifty million human beings; left hundreds of millions of others wounded in mind or body and materially devastated much of the heartland of civilization.[1]

World War II led to the Cold War; its effects dominated the world's economies and international politics for the remainder of the twentieth century. For my parents' generation and mine, World War II is simply "the war," but to my children and grandchildren it is an event of that long undifferentiated period called "history." I include, therefore, some relevant history to set the events of 1955–56 in context and evoke the ambiance of Munich at that time.

Pariah at War's End, 1945

Consider what thoughts the word "Germany" evoked for the people of the Western world in 1945:

Germany—whose half-mad leader Adolf Hitler plunged the world into the bloodiest war of all time and committed suicide before he could be brought to trial for his crimes.

Germany—the militaristic and aggressive power that instigated World War II and that, by repeated aggressions and threats of force, accomplished the *Anschluss* (annexation) of Austria to Germany; occupied Czechoslovakia; launched its *blitzkrieg* conquest of Poland, followed by the invasion and conquest of Holland, Belgium, Denmark, Norway, and France; and turned to attack Britain and the Soviet Union.

Germany—which declared war on the United States four days after the Japanese attack on Pearl Harbor and promptly turned its submarine forces against U.S. ships.

Germany—whose Luftwaffe (air force) introduced the horror of intentional bombing of civilian populations, as in Warsaw, Rotterdam, and London.

Germany—which carried out hate-filled persecutions and mass

---

1. John Keegan, foreword to *The Second World War* (New York: Penguin Books, 1989).

murders of six million European Jews, plus Gypsies, Communists, homosexuals, sick and handicapped persons, prisoners of war, and others, leaving the world with nightmarish additions to its experience and new words for its vocabulary, including "the Holocaust," "death camp," "gas chamber," and recollections of the atrocities committed at places like Dachau, Auschwitz, Treblinka, and Babi Yar.

Germany—whose descent into barbarism had made it by 1945 the most detested country of the world.

Devastated and Desperate at War's End

Germany surrendered unconditionally on May 8, 1945; its defeat was total and its condition desperate. This desperate condition is briefly and vividly described by Constantine Fitzgibbon in his book *Denazification*:

> The condition of that country, in the summer of 1945, was awful to behold: its cities in ruin, almost all its youthful and middle-aged men dead or in prisoner-of-war camps, its civilians close to starvation, every square yard of its territory occupied by its enemies, without a government of any sort while local administrative bodies functioned spasmodically or not at all, and, finally, itself an object of almost universal and fully justified detestation for the crimes that had been committed at Auschwitz and elsewhere by the Nazi rulers and by so many of their subjects. Perhaps not since the Romans' destruction of Carthage at the end of the Third Punic War had any great country of the West been so utterly smashed, militarily, economically and morally.[2]

Moreover, ethnic German refugees from Eastern Europe moved back to Germany on a colossal scale. They came in two phases: first was a flight before the advancing Red Army; second was the result of the Soviet Union's deliberate expulsion of Germans from areas where they had lived for centuries or even a thousand years, for example, Silesia, Czech Sudetenland, East Prussia, Poland, and the Baltic states. By 1946 the German population of Europe east of the Elbe River had been reduced by about 15 million people. Hundreds of thousands,

---

2. Constantine Fitzgibbon, *Denazification* (London: Michael Joseph, 1969), 9.

possibly a million, had died in the course of their journey.[3] This flood of German refugees joined millions of other displaced persons [DPs] in camps constructed to give them shelter in Germany.

Meanwhile, Stalin's armies kept a firm grip on all of East Europe and the Soviet Union and, despite promises of free elections, installed Communist governments throughout the area, making a Soviet bloc of nations uncooperative with, indeed even antagonistic to, the Western Allies.

The situation was made clear and given a name by Winston Churchill in his famous "Iron Curtain" speech at Westminster College in Fulton, Missouri, on March 5, 1946:

> From Stettin in the Baltic to Trieste in the Adriatic an iron curtain has descended across the Continent. Behind that line lie all the capitals of the ancient states of Central and Eastern Europe. Warsaw, Berlin, Prague, Vienna, Budapest, Belgrade, Bucharest and Sofia; all these famous cities and the populations around them lie in what I must call the Soviet sphere, and all are subject, in one form or another, not only to Soviet influence but to a very high and in some cases increasing measure of control from Moscow.[4]

The leaders of the victorious powers and the oppressed peoples of the countries formerly occupied by the German Army had little sympathy for Germany. In the United States, for example, Henry Morgenthau, secretary of the treasury and confidant of President Roosevelt, proposed a plan to turn Germany into an agricultural state, stripped of its industry and of all military powers. This plan was not adopted but it illustrates the Allies' deep feelings of anger against Germany.

The most dramatic and widely publicized action against the Germans was the Nuremberg War Crimes Trials of November 1945 to October 1946, during which the top leaders of the Nazi Party and government under Hitler were tried on charges of crimes against peace, war crimes, or crimes against humanity. Many more tribunals judged lesser soldiers or officials, and millions of Germans were required to register and provide information about their involvement, if any, with

---

3. Keegan, *Second World War*, 592.
4. Winston Churchill, "Iron Curtain Speech" (Westminster College, Fulton, MO, March 5, 1946), www.fordham.edu/halsall/mod/churchill-iron.html.

the Nazi Party or its infamous offspring like the SS, the SD, or the Gestapo (see the glossary).

How could this Germany, in just ten years, become an ally of the Western powers, a successful democracy, an economic powerhouse, a member of the North Atlantic Treaty Organization (NATO), and a contributor of soldiers, sailors, and airmen to NATO's defense of western Europe against the Soviet Union?

The Cold War Struggle over Germany

Historians will find many factors to explain the intensity of the German–Russian enmity: the two thousand years of struggles between Germanic and Slavonic tribes for the lands of northern Europe, the savagery of the German forces against the Russian population in its invasion of Russia in World War II, the equally savage retaliation of the Russian Army against the German population in its march to Berlin, the widespread fear in Germany and the rest of the West that Stalin intended to impose totalitarian Communism on Europe by force of arms, the uncooperative and even aggressive acts of the Soviet Union in the Four Power governing of Germany, and the spread of Communist governments, revolutions, and insurgencies in many parts of the world.

The Cold War arose from the conflicting interests of the Western Allies (principally the United States, Britain, and France) and the Soviet Union at the time of Germany's unconditional surrender in 1945. The contest spread worldwide and took on an ideological aspect of one-party Communism versus free democratic government and market capitalism. Traditional national power interests remained central, however, and Germany was the field upon which the contest centered; it was the epicenter of the Cold War.

Defeated Germany was occupied by the armed forces of the four victorious powers, each administering a zone, in other words, an area of Germany approximately the same as the German territory its armies had conquered. Both the Western Allies and the Soviet Union said they wanted a united Germany but each wanted a Germany united under its own hegemony. The Soviets especially wanted a united Germany under their control, for they shared a continent with the Germans. Uneasy neighbors, Slavs and Germans had struggled over control of central Europe for centuries and had fought major wars twice in the twentieth century. Poland was a buffer between the Germans and the Russians, but the Soviets had seen how quickly Hitler's army had defeated Poland and raced to the Russian border.

Stalin was convinced he could achieve his goal and go on to dominate Europe. With large and vigorous Communist parties in France and Italy, and the threatening presence of the giant Soviet Army in Eastern Europe, Stalin believed he could succeed by political pressure and threat of force without starting a new war.

The Soviets were realists, however, and understood that they would not win the support of the Germans living in the East Zone because of the traditional German-Slav antagonisms and because of the Red Army's brutality on entering Germany at the war's end. Inspired by General Zhukov's order to take revenge for the acts of the German forces in the Soviet Union, the Soviet soldiers burned and pillaged farms and towns and raped all the German women they found. "Estimates based on newly released documents and on contemporary records indicate that as many as two million German women were raped, sometimes repeatedly and in the most humiliating manner, and that all lived in dread of it," wrote W. R. Smyser in *From Yalta to Berlin*.[5] Millions of Germans fled west, abandoning their homes and lands. East of the Oder River the flight of the German population cleared the land that was to be given to Poland, but the raping, burning, and looting by the Russians west of the Oder served no strategic purpose; it served only to alienate the whole German nation. For many years, indeed decades, after the end of World War II, German women would not speak of the Soviets except with loathing.

The Western Allies responded to Soviet pressure in ways unexpected by the Kremlin. War weary though they were, the United States, Britain, and France rearmed and entered into the NATO alliance for defense of West Europe against the Soviet threat. And so the struggle for Germany went on for many years, a struggle in diplomacy, trade, economy, and military power. Overhanging all was the threat of mutual nuclear annihilation.

Munich and Bavaria in the 1950s

Munich had not been spared in the Allied air bombardments during the war. By the time I arrived in 1955, the city had been mostly repaired or rebuilt, with occasional half-standing buildings or empty lots as reminders of the war. Munich in the 1950s was a large and sophisticated city—a cultural center with palaces, museums, galleries, theaters,

---

5. W. R. Smyser, *From Yalta to Berlin: The Cold War Struggle over Germany* (New York: St. Martin's Griffin, 1999), 38.

churches, a famous university, and a *Technische Hochschule* (Institute of Technology). And Bavaria, proud of its past independence under the centuries-old rule of the Wittelsbach kings, held tight to its own traditions, its Catholicism, and its political conservatism.

Bavaria is a beautiful land of forests, lakes, and mountains. It is an ancient land, part of which lay within the Roman Empire, but most of which lay north of the borders of that world power. There is so much to see—the lakes: the Starnbergersee, Tegernsee, Chiemsee, the Königsee, Schliersee, Bodensee, and hundreds more; the mountains: the Bavarian Alps form the southern border of Germany with Switzerland and Austria; the clean and orderly towns and villages with their Maypoles and large sturdy houses with front balconies and windows adorned with flower boxes and paintings covering the triangular spaces from the entrance door to the peak of the roof over the entrance; the onion-domed baroque and rococo churches, monasteries, and nunneries; and lively people wearing traditional Bavarian attire, *dirndls* for the women, *lederhosen* for the men.

But all was not fun, art, education, music, and quaint folkways in Munich and Bavaria; the region's history had a dark side too. The Nazi Party was founded in Munich, and Hitler kept the party's headquarters there. The Nazis' first attempt to seize government power, the Bier Hall Putsch of 1923, took place in Munich. Hitler wrote *Mein Kampf* while he was in Bavaria's Landsberg Prison serving a term for his role in the attempted coup. Nuremberg is in Bavaria, and the infamous Nazi Party rally of 1935, the largest and most threatening rally of the Nazi movement, took place in Nuremberg. The first and one of the most infamous of the Nazis' death-dealing concentration camps, Dachau, was in Bavaria only a few miles from Munich.

Munich in the 1950s was a capital of the Cold War, an important city, crowded with German residents, German and Slavic refugees from the east, former slave laborers, and American soldiers. Radio Free Europe and Radio Liberty, America's two high-powered broadcasting stations targeted to East Europe, were located in or near Munich. The city itself was a jungle of competing secret intelligence organizations—British, French, American, Russian, East and West German, Czech, Polish, and more. Émigré organizations of Eastern European and Balkan states were also active in the struggle.

Life for most of Munich's residents flowed on quietly and safely, but beneath the calm everyday life of the city lay an intelligence jungle—kidnappings, defections, agents, and double agents. From time to time violence erupted in assassinations or attempted assassinations. For example, on March 27, 1952, a bomb hidden in a parcel addressed to Federal Chancellor Konrad Adenauer blew up in the basement of the police station in Munich, killing the expert technician who was opening the parcel. Four days later a second bomb arrived by post, addressed to the head of the German commission for negotiations with Israel on compensation, at The Hague. According to Gen. Reinhard Gehlen's book, *The Service*, in 1961 a KGB agent, Bogdan Stashinsky, turned himself in to the West Berlin police and confessed to assassinating two well-known Ukrainian politicians—Lev Rebet on October 12, 1957, and Stefan Bandera, a former Allied agent and leader of the anti-Communist group Organization of Ukrainian Nationalists (OUN), on October 15, 1959, both in Munich. Stashinsky explained that he had followed his victims and killed them with a poison-dart pistol provided to him by the KGB. This silent pistol fired a capsule of hydrogen cyanide into the victim's face, poisoning him immediately. A parcel addressed to the exiled politician Czermak (said to be an intelligence agent of the West) blew up at a Munich post office, killing its addressee. In September 1964 Horst Schwirkmann, a technician attached to the West German embassy in Moscow, was attacked by a sudden spray of mustard gas at short range, a poison designed to kill him within a few days, while leaving little trace of the cause. Schwirkmann was a technician trained to discover hidden microphones planted by the KGB in diplomatic buildings around the world. He was on the threshold of reporting their installation of thirty microphones in the German embassy in Moscow. Schwirkmann, seriously ill, was flown out of Moscow by the Germans and his life was saved by treatment in Germany.[6]

Return of Sovereignty to Germany in Phases

Germany was not transformed in a day. The process took more than ten years, from the end of the fighting in 1945 to Germany's recovery of full sovereignty, its membership in NATO, and the arrival of the first recruits to West German armed forces in 1956. The restoration of German sovereignty occurred in phases.

---

6. Reinhard Gehlen, *The Service: The Memoirs of General Reinhard Gehlen*, trans. David Irving (New York: World Publishing, 1972), 240–241, 262–263.

Phase 1: May 1945-1949, Military Government,
No German Sovereignty

From the time of its unconditional surrender in May 1945 until 1949 Germany had no national government and was under military rule by the four victorious powers—the United States, Britain, France, and the Soviet Union. On June 5, 1945, in a Berlin declaration, the four Allies assumed supreme powers in Germany, and during the Potsdam Conference of July 17–August 2, 1945, it was agreed that Germany would be divided into zones, each zone governed by the army of one of the victorious Allies, with an Allied Control Council made up of the commanding generals theoretically governing over all. In addition, Berlin, Germany's capital city, located deep within the Soviet zone, was divided into four sectors, one to each of the victors, also governed overall by the Allied Control Council.

These arrangements did not work as intended; there were serious conflicts between the three Western Allies and the Soviet Union. Consequently, the Western Allies united their zones into one economic zone, and on June 20–21, 1948, to fight serious inflation, carried out a currency reform, issuing a new currency for West Germany, the *Deutschmark.*

The currency reform of 1948 and the arrival of economic assistance from America's Marshall Plan started West Germany on the road to economic recovery. Every aspect of the economy seemed to grow and West Germany became a major engine of European growth. The Korean War provided further stimulus as West German industry filled demands for products needed by the United States and other nations to replace American production diverted to war needs. West Germany's economy rose rapidly from the stagnation and destruction left by World War II and was admired all over the world as the *Wirtschaftswunder* (economic miracle). By the time I arrived in 1955, West Germany was prosperous but not yet completely recovered.

In retaliation for the currency reform, the Soviet Union almost immediately (on June 24, 1948) started its blockade of Berlin, an attempt to drive the Western Allies out of the city. And in response, within the first two days of the blockade, the Western Allies launched the Berlin airlift to provide food and fuel for the city. The blockade and the airlift lasted until May 12, 1949—almost a year of high tension and risk of war.

Phase 2: 1949-1954, Partial Sovereignty in West Germany,
Federal Republic Established
In 1949 the Western Allies granted a partial return of sovereignty to a
newly created Federal Republic of Germany (Bundesrepublik
Deutschland), which in the course of 1949 adopted a Basic Law
(*Grundgesetz*), effectively a constitution (May 23); elected a parlia-
ment (*Bundestag*) (August 14); elected Theodor Heuss as president
(September 12); and elected Konrad Adenauer as chancellor (Sep-
tember 15). Putting into effect the changes creating the new Federal
Republic took some months and extended into 1950.

The Soviets responded by formally establishing the German Democratic Republic (Deutsche Demokratische Republik, or DDR) in the
Soviet occupation zone (October 7, 1949).

From its establishment in 1949–50 until 1955, the Federal Republic (West Germany) governed itself in internal affairs, but authority over military and foreign affairs remained in the hands of the Western Allies. The occupying troops of the Western allies remained by
agreement of the Federal Republic and the three Western powers.
The defunct Allied Control Council of generals was replaced by an
Allied High Commission whose members were civilians.

Phase 3: 1954-55, Full Sovereignty Returned to Federal Republic
Finally, in 1954–55, the Federal Republic regained full sovereignty,
joined the NATO alliance, and began rearming. It also negotiated
recognition by the Soviet Union, the return of German prisoners of
war still incarcerated in the USSR, and the continued presence of the
NATO powers' armed forces. Implementation of these matters was
rapid, and in 1956 the Federal Republic had ministries of defense and
of foreign affairs and the first group of recruits put on the uniforms of
the new German armed forces. German officers were selected for important positions in NATO.

In 1955 and 1956 the common hopes of the United States and
Germany as to Germany's future role in Europe came to fruition. These
years saw the completion of Germany's transformation from enemy
to ally.

PART 1

THE MYSTERY OFFICE IN MUNICH

1

A PRE-DAWN DRIVE TO AIR BASE FÜRSTENFELDBRUCK

I drove the black Mercedes slowly through the pre-dawn darkness of Munich, following carefully the directions given to me again in my wake-up call from CDR Val Rychly, whom most of us called "the Skipper." The streets were empty at this early hour and the street lights managed only to mark out yellow circles in the surrounding black, until, driving south on the Tegernseer Landstrasse, I passed the brightly lit prison-like walls of McGraw Kaserne—a former German Army base and barracks. I took a right turn into the Nauplia Strasse and then drove straight ahead, across Geiselgasteig and into the darkness of the tree-lined Gabriel Max Strasse.

In the dark, the big houses lining the street looked much alike, but a small light marked the driveway entrance to the Skipper's house. I slowed, shifted down, and turned left into the rising driveway. I stopped at the top in front of the door of the house. I was pleased with myself for I had never before been to this house and had found my way with no mistakes. The front door opened at once and the Skipper came out. He was in civilian clothes and carried a suitcase. We put his suitcase in the trunk, and he took the front seat beside me and said, "Good morning . . . right on time. Now to pick up our passenger. I'll guide you there."

We were soon out of Munich on a main highway heading southwest toward Starnberg. There was almost no traffic, just an occasional long distance truck with bright headlights that bored holes in the darkness but were diverted down when approaching us. It wasn't far to Starnberg, and after a few minutes the Skipper directed me to turn off the highway onto a paved suburban road leading through an area of fields and woods to a community of well-kept middle-class houses. We stopped before a house, the Skipper went to the door and almost

13

immediately came back accompanied by a thin man of medium height wearing a topcoat with the collar turned up, a scarf around his neck, and a hat with the brim pulled down in front. In the darkness I saw little of his face. The Skipper introduced me to "Doktor Schneider" and told him that I was "Leutnant Durning," his assistant in the U.S. Navy's Munich office, and that I would drive them to the U.S. Air Force base at Fürstenfeldbruck. I put Doktor Schneider's suitcase in the car's trunk alongside the Skipper's, while they took their places in the back seat of the car.

The Skipper had mapped out the route to the air base at Fürstenfeldbruck, a former German Luftwaffe base about ten or fifteen miles west of Munich. We arrived at the lighted gate to the air base and stopped at the barrier. Two armed military guards came out of the gatehouse, shined a flashlight at the German license plate on our German-make car and looked concerned. I rolled down my window and showed my Navy ID card to one of the guards. While he examined it, the Skipper stepped out of the car and handed the other guard an envelope containing a letter from the base commander authorizing our entrance. Both guards read the letter, and one carried it back into the gatehouse and placed a telephone call. While he spoke on the telephone, his colleague searched our car thoroughly, examined our ID cards, including the German civilian ID issued by the German police to Doktor Schneider, and shined his flashlight on our faces to compare with the photos on our cards. This took only a few minutes and the first guard returned from the gatehouse, spoke quietly to his colleague, and then said, "You must wait a few minutes until an officer of the watch arrives to authorize your entry and guide you to your destination." Almost immediately a jeep arrived with a U.S. Air Force officer and driver. The officer took the letter that the Skipper had presented, read it carefully, put it in a briefcase he carried, and said, "Welcome, Gentlemen. Please follow my jeep. Please do not fall behind, stop, or turn off."

The rest was easy. The gate was raised and we drove through. We followed the jeep past a cluster of buildings and then out onto the paved area in front of a line of hangars. We stopped alongside a white two-engine U.S. Navy plane that was warming its engines and going through standard tests in preparation for takeoff. I stopped the car near the plane and took the suitcases from the trunk. As I looked up, the pilot, a U.S. Navy officer, came out of the plane, welcomed his passengers, and took them and their suitcases aboard. I waited until the plane taxied away, then followed the jeep back to the gate and drove back to Munich.

A dramatic dawn was breaking, and I felt exhilarated. Everything had gone exactly as planned. It was a good start to an important trip that would strengthen German ties with the United States and its NATO allies. In the quiet and beauty of the morning, lulled by the steady hum of the car's engine, my mind called up vivid memories of the events of the months since receiving my orders to duty in Germany. I remembered my arrival in Munich.

2

TO GERMANY AND TO MUNICH

Arrival in Munich

The train car swayed as it rolled through the long maze of tracks, signal lights, and switches, cutting its way through the dark rail yard to the main station. It was a cold night; out of the window I saw only a gray white curtain of falling snow, occasionally interrupted by the blurry orange or green glow of a signal light. I shivered a little from my memory of Munich as the Nazi Party's birthplace and my recollection of the empty, evasive "briefings" I had received about my forthcoming duties here.

It was February 21, 1955, almost a decade since the end of World War II in Europe, three decades since Adolf Hitler, a fanatic little Austrian-turned-German superpatriot, launched his brutal Nazi Party in this city.

"München Hauptbahnhof! . . . München Hauptbahnhof!" (Munich main station!)

The conductor's sharp cry brought me suddenly full awake. The train slowed and stopped at the station. Then came another call directing us to leave the train.

"Alle austeigen! Austeigen, bitte!" (Everyone out, please!) The *bitte* seemed perfunctory; the tone was one of command. I pulled my bag from the overhead rack, maneuvered it clumsily down the aisle, and stepped onto the platform. Stung by the sharp cold and surprised by the feel of falling snow, I looked up—and understood. The frame of the great barrel-shaped roof of the station was only partially in place and the roof itself was gone—a reminder of the thoroughness of the Allied air bombardment of Germany's rail system—rolling stock, stations, bridges, yards, and surrounding areas. Wondering how I would find the Navy contact promised me at Heidelberg, I started down the platform to the gate.

16

At the end of the platform, a young American in blue jeans and a heavy quilted jacket stepped forward with a smile and a softly spoken, Southern-accented query—"Mr. Durning?" It was Yeoman First Joseph Foster (not his real name). Spotting me had been easy; he said, "Not many U.S. Navy officers in uniform arrive at the Munich train station." Joe put my bag in the back of a gray Navy pickup. I climbed in up front and we drove away, crossing the Bahnhof Platz, the large and empty square in front of the station, and turning onto a street lined by buildings in varying states of repair. Through the falling snowflakes I saw scaffold-covered buildings lighted by powerful flood lamps. On the scaffolds were German workers, in heavy coats, gloves, and hard hats, vigorously at work restoring the buildings. I soon learned that they worked around the clock, even in the snowfall. They were my vivid introduction to the miracle of the German economy, the *Wirtschaftswunder*.

Joe took me a few blocks farther to the Park Hotel, the U.S. Army's hotel for transient officers, and helped me with my bag. Then he turned to me, "Commander Rychly—we call him 'the Skipper'—sends his greetings and asks you to meet him tomorrow morning at the office. Tomorrow is a U.S. holiday and the office is closed, but the Skipper will be there. He asks that you come to the office tomorrow morning at 10. I'll pick you up here at 9:30."

The 1930s-looking hotel lobby was small, clean, but somewhat worn. A smiling blonde woman in her thirties, with a warm voice and a German accent, was behind the reception desk. "Good evening, sir, may I help you?"

Orders and Briefings

The room and the bed were adequate, but I couldn't sleep. Like flashbacks in a movie, my thoughts played back the events of the last thirty days. My orders, written in the Navy's traditional style, told me where I was to go and to whom to report but said nothing of what I was to do:

17 January 1955
From: Commandant, Eleventh Naval District
To: LTJG Marvin Bresler Durning, USNR, 474092/1105

[You are] detached from temporary duty and from such other duty which may have been assigned. Proceed to Washington, D.C., and upon arrival report to the Chief of Naval Operations, Navy Department, for temporary duty for about two (2) weeks. Upon completion of temporary duty and when directed by the Chief of Naval Operations, detached from temporary duty and from such other duty which may have been assigned. Proceed via such transportation as the Chief of Naval Personnel may designate to Heidelberg, Germany, and upon arrival report to Commander U.S. Naval Forces, Germany for duty on his staff.

My temporary duty at the Chief of Naval Operations (CNO) was for briefing at the Office of Naval Intelligence (ONI) in the Pentagon, a soulless building as big as a city and without a street map. Fortunately, I was generally familiar with the building's system of concentric five-sided floors, called "rings," which had corridors parallel to the exterior walls and shorter corridors at intervals radiating from the innermost to the outermost rings. Even with this head start it was a chore to find the CNO duty offices in order to report my arrival. Once there, I was logged in and directed to report to the ONI personnel office. That was easier to find because I had served in ONI in OP 921E, the section charged with protection of the Navy against sabotage, espionage, and subversion. At the ONI personnel office I learned that I was to serve in the Munich intelligence office of the Commander Naval Forces Germany (COMNAVGER). Naturally I wondered why the Navy had an intelligence office in Munich, an inland city, hundreds of miles from salt water.

For the next two weeks I was sent from office to office for briefing in the Pentagon and at ONI's Science and Technology Branch (S&T) on the grounds of the Naval Observatory on Massachusetts Avenue near Embassy Row. The briefings were general in nature beginning with the composition of U.S. Naval Forces in Germany, including the headquarters and Rhine River Patrol based at Heidelberg, the port facilities at Bremerhaven, and the intelligence offices in Frankfurt, Berlin, and Munich. Day after day I read or was told about Soviet bloc naval forces, their merchant shipping, their home ports, shipbuilding and repair facilities, and personnel training. An impressive group of very competent intelligence officers conducted the briefings, but they never said a word about what I was to do in Munich. Were they holding back or were they as much in the dark as I was?

And then came an intriguing visit to Jack Alberti in his office down the corridor from the Office of the Director of Naval Intelligence

(DNI). I had heard of Jack Alberti during my previous ONI service, but only as an important civilian whose duties at ONI were simply a mystery, a secret that I had no "need to know." His door was closed when I arrived, and nothing identified the room but its number in a standard Pentagon placard beside the door. I knocked and a man's voice invited me to enter. In the room, standing behind a standard Navy gray metal desk was a tall man in his forties, in a dark blue suit, with dramatic black hair, a light complexion, and a slight accent of some Mediterranean origin. He was a large, impressive man, dressed like a corporate chief executive, not a Navy civil servant. He exuded an air of authority.

The room was small and the furniture spare—the desk, a swivel chair, two gray metal file cabinets, and two straight chairs—all standard government issue, found in thousands of U.S. government offices all over the world. On the desk was a telephone but not a scrap of paper. It crossed my mind that he had cleared his desk and put all papers out of sight in preparation for my visit.

My time with Mr. Alberti was brief. I sat opposite him across his desk. He congratulated me on my good fortune of being assigned duty in Munich. After this, however, his demeanor became very serious and his eyes focused intently on my face:

> You will serve under Vladimir Rychly in Munich. You are fortunate; he is an outstanding intelligence officer. He is different, of course, from the usual U.S. naval officer—he grew up in central Europe, speaks many languages, including Russian. He has the intuitions of a cat—always wary, never off guard—but he takes chances when the stakes are worth it. Some years ago I had to work like the devil to prevent his arrest by U.S. Customs officials at National Airport on his arrival from Europe carrying a box of precious jewels. Customs wanted to hold him on suspicion of smuggling. He wasn't smuggling, of course, but, at the owners' request, carrying some of the crown jewels of a Balkan monarchy to the United States for safe-keeping—part of an important and secret intelligence matter. But sometimes people with little imagination don't understand Val Rychly. You have imagination, don't you, Mr. Durning? Keep your eyes open and listen carefully to Val Rychly. You will learn.

With that, my briefing ended. I left Jack Alberti's office with a tingle up my spine but still no idea of what I was to do in Munich.

Military Air to Germany

I traveled from Washington, D.C., to Germany via the Military Air Transport Service (MATS). The trip from National Airport to Rhein-Main Air Base near Frankfurt was uneventful but still exciting for me. The four engine plane was fitted out like a commercial passenger plane, with cushioned seats, a far cry from the two-engine Navy DC-3 of "FLOGWING" (the Fleet Logistic Air Wing) in which I had flown from island to island from Hawaii to Japan to meet my ship in my prior duty assignment.

The MATS flight over the Atlantic was accomplished in several steps: The first was from Washington, D.C., northeastward along the North American coast to an air base at Argentia, Newfoundland. The plane, filled with military personnel and dependents, arrived at Argentia around midnight. The night was crisp and cold. The sky was clear and sparkling with stars, while the earth about the air base was completely dark. Only the colored runway lights and yellow glow escaping a hangar-shaped building gave evidence of human presence. It was as if the air base were on the moon.

All passengers were required to leave the plane while it was refueled, but we were "refueled" as well. We were served a delicious steak dinner in a dining hall in the brightly lighted building. After about an hour we reboarded the plane for the second leg of our trip, southeastward across the Atlantic from Newfoundland to a U.S. air base in the Azores Islands. We arrived in the bright morning sunshine, in a warm and colorful world. The plane was again refueled, this time for its journey to Europe and the U.S. Rhein-Main Air Force Base. A hand-written endorsement on my orders stated that I arrived at the "Air Traf. Center, Frankfurt 16 2 55 at 1900 hrs" (February 16, 1955, at 7:00 p.m.).

The trip by U.S. military bus from the air base to the offices of COMNAVGER in Heidelberg was a slow one on a wet two-lane asphalt road, passing snow-covered fields under the heavy gray clouds of a north European winter. After about two hours, we reached Heidelberg, the headquarters of U.S. military forces in Germany. The bus made several stops to deliver passengers to Army buildings after which I was the only remaining passenger. I had to remind the driver of my presence and destination. It was late and the night was dark; the driver seemed uncertain where to go, but after conferring with a military police officer (MP), we set off again and finally stopped before the entrance of a long, drab two-story building, set among a number of similar buildings with high peaked roofs, perhaps former German army barracks. Carrying my suitcase, I entered the building and found a sole guard seated behind a desk in the entrance hall. I inquired as to the location of the COMNAVGER duty office, went there, and was sent across a small yard to a nearby Army bachelor officers quarters (BOQ), where at last I got some sleep.

Reporting at COMNAVGER

I was up very early the next morning, eager to report for duty. Promptly at 8:00 a.m. on February 17, 1955, I entered the COMNAVGER duty office and reported to the officer of the watch. At the direction of the watch officer, a yeoman took a copy of my orders, logged me in, and directed me down a long hall to the administrative offices, saying he would call ahead to alert them of my arrival. Nervous and excited, I walked as directed to the end of the hall, entered the room, identified myself to the yeoman behind the first desk, and was ushered into the adjacent office of Commander Worthington (not his real name, which I have forgotten). I announced myself in the traditional Navy fashion, "Lieutenant JG Marvin Durning reporting for duty, Sir," and received the traditional response, "Welcome aboard, Mr. Durning." Commander Worthington was informal but still observed familiar Navy courtesies. "So far, so good," I thought.

After some small talk about my trip from Washington to Heidelberg, the commander turned to business:

> We've been expecting you and have made some plans, I have an appointment for you to meet Admiral Harlfinger, our Commanding Officer, in a few minutes. I have called our Berlin, Frankfurt, and Munich intelligence offices and have a schedule for you to meet everyone and hear what they are up to. It's important that you meet everyone. It helps with personal relations and cooperation. It's especially important that you go to Berlin and meet Captain Day, for he is the Intelligence Officer for COMNAVGER. Your immediate superior officer in Munich will be Lieutenant Commander Rychly. He is Assistant Intelligence Officer and COMNAVGER representative in Munich. You'll leave this afternoon by car for a brief visit at the Frankfurt office, then on to the airfield for your flight by government air to Berlin. It is best you make these visits now, before you go to Munich.

Handing me my orders for temporary additional duty (TAD) in Berlin, Commander Worthington continued, "You'll have a few days in Berlin and will then come back here. We'll send you on by train to Munich." The commander's telephone rang, and while he took the call, I quickly scanned the TAD orders, which were dated February 17, 1955:

From: Commander, U.S. Naval Forces, Germany
To: LTJG Marvin Bresler DURNING, USNR 474092, 1105
Subj: Temporary Additional Duty

1. Proceed on or about 17 February 1955 to the place (or places in the order given) indicated below for temporary duty. This is in addition to your present duties and upon completion thereof you will return to your station and resume your regular duties:
    BERLIN, Germany, in connection with COMNAVGER instructions for a period of about 3 days, returning on or about 20 February 1955.
In the execution of these orders you are authorized to proceed by Government Vehicle and/or Government Rail and Air. Your clearance number for Berlin is 2 233.

The commander's telephone call was from the Frankfurt office; it was confirmed that I would leave early from Heidelberg in a Navy car. The driver would take me to the Frankfurt office, wait while I made a brief visit, then take me on to Rhein-Main Air Base.

The telephone rang again. The admiral would see me now. Commander Worthington led me to an office where he introduced me to Admiral Harlfinger, the commander of U.S. Naval Forces in Germany, on whose staff I was an "assistant intelligence officer" assigned to the Munich office. The meeting was brief; the admiral welcomed me aboard and wished me luck in my new duties, without telling me what they were.

My visit at the Frankfurt office lasted less than an hour, long enough for me to learn that the office was directed at S&T and was largely concerned with collecting German and other European technical journals and articles, following development of hydrofoil boats in Europe, research on "cavitation" of marine propellers, and similar matters of interest to the Navy. The two officers I met were open and friendly and told me that they occasionally conferred with Pete Aschenfelter, "the S&T officer in Munich." That was all I learned of Munich, however, and I was soon back in the car and off to Rhein-Main for my flight to Berlin.

To Berlin—Briefings and the Art Students' Ball

It was another typical North European winter day. From the plane I could see nothing but clouds below me. I was elated to learn I was going to Berlin. Thoughts and images raced through my mind: Hitler's capital . . . the siege of Berlin . . . behind the Iron Curtain . . . the Berlin Blockade and Allied Airlift . . . flashpoint of the Cold War . . . site of intelligence wars.

As had millions of others throughout the world, I had watched newsreels of the dramatic fight against the blockade and cheered the airmen who risked their lives with every flight and broke the blockade, teaching the Soviets a lesson about U.S. and British airpower and perseverance. And now I was seated in a U.S. military plane, flying through one of the same corridors flown by thousands of planes during the airlift, over the same Soviet occupied zone, now called the Deutsche Demokratische Republik (DDR). I was on my way to Berlin—or at least West Berlin, an island of freedom locked behind the Iron Curtain.

It was already dark in Berlin when the plane landed at about 7:30 p.m. The Army provided me with transportation to a BOQ, an attractive, modern white building surrounded by trees and snow-covered lawns. My room was luxurious compared to the usual Army or Navy barracks-BOQ room, more like a hotel, and it had been cleaned and polished until it shined. Early the next morning, per my instructions, I telephoned the Navy's intelligence office, and a car was sent to fetch me.

Allied bombing or Soviet artillery had destroyed much of Berlin, and there were still some empty lots and occasional, neatly stacked piles of debris, divided into bricks and stones. There were also many new buildings, and construction was under way everywhere; giant cranes dominated the skyline of West Berlin in every direction.

The Navy intelligence offices were in a modern office building. Upon arrival, I reported at the reception desk and was escorted to Captain Day's office. My reception was cordial. After the traditional Navy " . . . reporting for duty, Sir" on my part and the "Welcome aboard" response, Captain Day invited me to be seated, called for coffee for the two of us, and inquired as to my flight and the adequacy of my room at the BOQ.

Captain Day was in his forties and handsome in his uniform, which was adorned with shining gold stripes and service medals. He asked about my previous duties in the Navy, especially my time at ONI, and he was keenly interested in the extent and nature of my briefing in Washington; he seemed to want to help me get off to a good start. Because it was Friday, and my briefing could take more than one day, I would have to stay over the weekend. He noted with a smile that there might be a few things of interest for a young officer to see or do during his first visit to Berlin. In addition, he and his wife hoped I would be their guest for lunch on Saturday. For further orientation and briefing he would turn me over to Lieutenant Junior Grade Christianson (not his real name).

I liked Captain Day. I kept waiting for him to tell me more about Munich and my duties there, but he said only that it was a beautiful city and that Commander Rychly would be very glad to see me as he was short one officer already and a second would be leaving soon.

Captain Day led me to an adjacent room and introduced me to Lieutenant Junior Grade Christianson. Mr. Christianson was about my age, twenty-five, and the owner of a bright red MG sports convertible. In his briefing his tone was strictly professional. He said and did nothing overtly negative, but after Captain Day's warmth Mr. Christianson seemed cool. At first I thought that it was my imagination or the lieutenant's natural Scandinavian reserve, but as the day progressed his remarks took on a cutting edge and I sensed some anger or resentment against Commander Rychly and the Munich office. Mr. Christianson explained in a careful and guarded manner the flow of Soviet bloc (mostly East German) defectors or displaced persons into West Berlin and the Berlin office's interrogations of border crossers who might have information of interest to the Navy. He stressed the large number of border crossers from East to West Berlin, and the many hours or days needed to conduct one interrogation and write an accurate report. The Berlin office did other things, as well, but nothing especially exciting.

To my surprise, Christianson asked me whether Captain Day had told me anything about Commander Rychly and the Munich office's activities or its bad relations with Captain Day. I replied that no one, including Captain Day, had told me anything about the Munich office's activities, or my duties there, and that no one had said anything about bad relations. Christianson seemed annoyed, even angry: "That's the trouble: no one says anything, but there's something wrong. They must be doing more things than we know about, and Rychly must have direct ties to Washington, going around Captain Day. And, the reports they do send to Washington through us are just too numerous, too good for a small office in Munich to do. It makes me mad; they shouldn't treat Captain Day that way."

I said nothing. Christianson's loyalty to Captain Day was evident and admirable, but his anger, tinged perhaps by some envy, was an alert to possible problems and fuel for my already burning curiosity about my future duties. But I kept silent again; in my mind, I heard Jack Alberti's voice saying that Val Rychly was "different, of course, from the usual U.S. naval officer. . . . Keep your eyes open and listen carefully to Val Rychly. You will learn."

Christianson said, apologetically, that he could not show me around Berlin because he had other commitments, but he briefed me with enthusiasm on some other interesting aspects of life in Berlin. First in order of importance was that attractive young German women were in abundance in Berlin, which had a scarcity of young German men caused, of course, by the heavy losses of World War II. Life was drab for the many young German women in the city. Social life was easy, however, for a young American officer with a bright red sports car and some dollars in his pocket. Indeed, with a rare display of humor Christianson told me an easy way to meet German girls. "Just park your sports car along a busy street with the top down; go away for a while, then come back and throw out the girls you don't want."

He also strongly recommended that I attend the annual Berlin art students' ball, that year called *Schräger Zinnober* (Slanted Vermillion, a nonsense name), that was to be held Saturday night. It was by reputation Berlin's most famous costume party and an escape from the grim North German winter into a naughty revelry. To my concerns that I had no costume and no date, he said I should not worry, "Wear your civilian suit; they'll decorate you somehow with crepe paper and give you a mask. And don't worry about a date; you'll meet someone there. The rule is that couples must separate at the door and not meet again until midnight. If you want to see something of the real Berlin you shouldn't miss this chance to see the art students' ball." I was persuaded.

The next day, Saturday, was very cold and snow was falling. After breakfast I returned to my BOQ room where I spent some pleasant time reading about German history before my lunch appointment. Captain Day arrived at the BOQ at noon and drove me to his home in the elegant, wooded suburb of Dahlem. I met Mrs. Day and had sherry, and then we drove to an officers club for lunch. Mrs. Day was a friendly, attractive Southern lady who was pleased to learn that I had grown up in New Orleans, and she quickly put me at ease with stories of life in four-power Berlin. The lunch was excellent in all ways. Back at the BOQ I marveled at the warm reception I had received from Captain and Mrs. Day. It was only mid-afternoon so I settled in again with my books on German history.

That evening I took a taxi to *Schräger Zinnober*. The ball was in a huge museum-like building. I went in my civilian suit and explained that I was costumed as an American tourist. The students selling tickets at the door were good-natured and thought my costume fine, needing only a touch of color. A young woman dressed as a pirate took me aside, tied a giant bow tie of red crepe paper around my neck, and put a black mask over my eyes and nose. Then she stepped back, surveyed her handiwork, and said I was now a very good imitation of an American tourist, and standing just inside the entrance door, she added, "Also . . . bitte, kommen Sie herein, Amerikanischer Turist" (OK, please come in, American tourist).

Entering the building through a dimly lighted marble hallway lined with statues, I came to a slightly brighter marble room where a band was playing American big band swing music. In an alcove between two large sculptures was a bar. A large crowd of young people almost filled the room leaving only a dance space in the middle. Some couples were dancing, and others were standing around talking and drinking *Sekt*, the German cousin of champagne. Still others were walking around the room observing the scene. Sometimes a lone man or woman would approach someone and ask him or her to dance. I never saw anyone refuse, so I got up my courage and asked a masked young woman in a harem costume to dance. In my halting German and her halting English we were able to accomplish some small talk, and we stayed together for another dance. Then we both said, "*danke*" (thanks), and went our different ways.

I noticed couples leaving the ballroom, walking, often hand in hand, down one or another of several long corridors and decided to explore more of the building myself. I should have known better, for the hallways were very dimly lit and between or behind almost all the statues or other sculptures were amorous couples getting to know each other much better. I returned to the ballroom and to the most memorable episode of the occasion.

During my exploration down the hall, a small commotion had begun in the ballroom. A truly beautiful young blonde woman had arrived. Except for the long blonde hair hanging down her back, she was nude to the waist, and below her waist she wore a Polynesian grass skirt that she somehow kept in swaying motion, revealing her long legs. She was covered from head to toe with some powder or lotion which gave her the look of a deep suntan. In truth, she was breathtaking, and men were lined up to dance with her. She was poised, graceful, almost regal, as she danced and smiled at her partners. Naturally, I watched for a while, but I didn't have the courage to join that long line waiting to dance with her. In my mind I named her the Queen of the Ball.

I spent Sunday sleeping, reading, and recovering from *Schräger Zinnober*.

To Munich

On Monday I returned to Heidelberg and reported to Commander Worthington on my stop in Frankfurt and my trip to Berlin, including Captain Day's warm hospitality. Commander Worthington was pleased that all had gone well. My Berlin orders were endorsed, and I received new orders for travel to Munich that afternoon.

I was taken to the Heidelberg train station in a Navy car. The train, as always in Germany, arrived exactly on time. I climbed aboard, found an empty compartment, lifted my suitcase onto the rack above my head, and settled down for the trip to Munich. The day was dark and cold; snow covered the ground. I could see little out of the window except dark forests and increasing mists. I needed time to think over all that had happened and not happened. Why was everything about the Munich office so secret? What was so "different" about Commander Rychly and the Munich office? Why had no one in ONI or in Germany told me anything about the Munich office's work or my duties there? Did they know anything themselves? Perhaps they had no "need to know." The words of Jack Alberti ran through my mind. I could hear his voice as if I were sitting in his office: "Vladimir Rychly . . . is an outstanding intelligence officer. He is different. . . . Keep your eyes open and listen carefully to Val Rychly. You will learn."

Need to Know

"Need to know" is a fundamental rule of intelligence security, repeated so often in my training that it became almost a sacred invocation, a mantra to protect our secrets and ourselves. "Need to know" works both ways: he who needs to know something to perform his duties should be told, but nothing should be shared with him who has no need to know. Fortunately, this rule had been drilled into me during my first Navy assignment, my work in the Pentagon in the Office of Naval Intelligence, OP 921E. I worked first on the Navy's program screening naval personnel under the government-wide loyalty-security program and then as analyst of information possibly affecting the security of naval personnel, ships, or facilities in the Far East area. In both assignments I worked alone, reporting to the head of OP 921E or his deputy but having no discussion about my work with my office colleagues.

In all my briefings—in Washington, D.C., Heidelberg, Frankfurt, and Berlin—I had learned that Munich and Commander Rychly were somehow different from the other offices and officers but nothing more. I had heard not one word about what activities were carried out in the Munich office or about what my duties would be. I could understand this curtain of silence only if I believed those briefing me knew nothing themselves about the Munich office; they had no "need to know."

I looked forward to meeting Commander Rychly in the morning. At last I might learn what others did not tell me.

3

VAL RYCHLY, "THE SKIPPER"

The big house on Gabriel Max Strasse was still and dark, visible only by the dim moonlight reflecting off the snow around it.

Val Rychly was tired. His meeting with the admirals had lasted until 2:00 a.m. It had been a good meeting, full of important discussions, and he had stayed up another hour to write a first draft of his report. He was not only tired; he felt feverish. But he knew he must go to his office to meet the new officer who had just arrived. Durning was his name. Was that a German name? Durnin, perhaps, but changed in America?

Rychly heard noises from the kitchen as he dressed. He felt a little better. Frau Mattheus, his housekeeper, was up and dressed and making coffee for him and his guests. She was bossy at times, but she "ran a taut ship," supervised the part-time cook and maids, greeted his guests in German, French, or English, and was completely discreet. Pete Aschenfelter and Charlie O'Hearn didn't like her, but they just didn't understand.

He dressed for the day and went to the kitchen, where he exchanged "*Guten morgens*" (Good mornings) with Frau Mattheus and received a tumultuous, wiggling, trembling, barking, licking, joyous greeting from his three little dachshunds (called *dachls* familiarly in Bavaria)— Ickie, Jochl, and Ami. He held, petted, and talked to each in turn, reassuring each by his touch and the sound of his voice, then filled their dishes with their morning food. Watching their antics and their rush to their dishes, he felt better at once, even though he had the achy joints, watery eyes, and sniffles of an oncoming head cold or flu.

The dachls were great friends and pets, but they were also prize winning competitors at dog shows around Bavaria. They had won over Frau Mattheus as well, and she smiled as she watched the morning ritual of their joyous reunion with Val. She approved of their pedigree and of the "*gute gebildete Leute*" (the right kind of people) they met at the dog shows.

Frau Mattheus, Mrs. Matthews in English and frequently "Pat" inside the household, was in her sixties. She was from a formerly well-to-do family in Frankfurt, a family that had owned hotels before the war but had lost everything in the British and American bombing attacks during the war. She had an excellent education, was fluent in German, French, and English, and was accustomed to managing servants and graciously providing for groups of guests, all in the strict old fashioned ways of Germany's pre–World War I upper-middle class. She was a widow left in desperate straits by the destruction of the family's hotels. She had a brother in Frankfurt, but he was equally destitute and unable to support her.

Her luck changed when she answered an advertisement in a German newspaper from an American military officer seeking a general housekeeper. Her qualifications were outstanding, even if she was a bit stern in her demeanor. After discreet checks on her background through the Army's Counterintelligence Corps and German police records, Val hired her. The choice was inspired, for her old-fashioned and conservative ways were just right to make his German guests feel at home during their frequent visits. Frau Mattheus was forever grateful and loyal to Val Rychly. She repeated often that she had nothing and nowhere to go when Val hired her, an event she described as the time when Val "took her in" and "gave her a home again."

During his breakfast Val thought of the day ahead. "I asked Durning to come into the office so I could meet him. What would this new officer be like? He was young, only in his twenties, but he reportedly spoke some German and had intelligence experience from his earlier duty at ONI. Maybe this time my luck has changed and I'll get some help on the sensitive work. But I must be careful, bring Durning along slowly, watch him, see first how he gets on with the Germans at the office. Then maybe I'll introduce him to more."

Meeting Commander Rychly at Last

By 9:00 a.m. it was a bright winter day, and sunlight fell on the clean new snow. Joe was right on time, and I climbed into the Navy car, hoping that the glorious weather was an omen of good things to come. I was excited and watched carefully, noting the beauty of the Bavarian capital. The drive to the office was short but impressive. We passed the palace of the Wittelsbachs, the last monarchs of once-independent Bavaria, and great stone buildings lining the Prinzregenten Strasse. We traveled over the Isar River and around the Friedensengel, a tower topped by a heroic statue of the Angel of Peace, and continued on the Äussere (outer) Prinzregenten Strasse to a square dominated on the right by the gray stone hulk of the Bavarian State Opera. Then we turned left for several blocks on the Possart Strasse, a residential street; then right at the Possart Platz, a quiet, wooded, snow-bedecked square surrounded by stately homes. Joe pointed across the square to an especially large and handsome house surrounded by snow-covered gardens, a mansion with grounds that covered most of the block on which it stood. "There it is, Mr. Durning, our offices—Possart Platz 3. Commander Rychly—the Skipper—is already here, and we are right on time."

Joe turned left around the square and into the curved driveway entrance to the big house at Possart Platz 3. He had keys to the house. We entered through a short foyer and hall to a large reception area in the center of the house with an atrium rising to the third floor and an elegant stairway wrapping gracefully around the atrium to the second and then to the third floor. Everything was glistening clean and orderly. The outside of the house had impressed me, and the inside widened my eyes still more. Possart Platz 3 reminded me of some embassies in Washington, D.C.; it bore no resemblance at all to the Navy's usual Spartan quarters.

Joe led me up the stairs to the second floor and into a foyer at the front of the house. In the foyer were three secretarial desks for the yeomen, and from it doors led to rooms both right and left. Joe took my Navy uniform topcoat and hung it in a closet, then stepped to the doorway to Commander Rychly's office. "Mr. Durning is here, Sir," said Joe.

"Send him in," came the reply in a husky voice.

In an instant the mystery about Commander Rychly and the activities of the Munich office that dominated my briefings flashed through my mind, leaving me both excited and cautious about finally meeting my new commanding officer. With my hat under my left arm, I stepped into the office and saw him standing behind a huge and elegant desk of dark wood. Standing at attention, I announced myself, Navy style:

"Lieutenant JG Marvin Durning, Sir, reporting for duty."

"Welcome aboard, Mr. Durning. We've been waiting for you. Here, sit in this chair across the desk from me, so we can talk."

Vladimir Rychly was in his forties, of more than average height, with touches of gray in his dark hair and a deep, husky voice. A crease ran down each cheek of his face, adding interest and distinction to his appearance. A slight, unusual accent to his words clearly indicated some non-American background, but it wasn't German, French, Italian, or any other inflection that I could recognize. He was dressed neatly in civilian clothes, including a handsome dark sweater. He explained, with an apology, that he felt as if he might be catching a cold or the flu. The ghost of a question raced by in my mind: Why was it important to drag himself in to meet me on a holiday, rather than wait another day?

Our conversation flowed easily as he asked me about myself, my hometown roots, my education, my previous duties at ONI and aboard a destroyer in the Pacific, and my command of German and French. Finally, gently, came the query: "Well, what did they tell you in your briefings about this office and your duties?"

"Almost nothing," I replied. Then I told him briefly of the content of my ONI, Heidelberg, Frankfurt, and Berlin briefings. "The only thing I learned was that you were the commanding officer in Munich and had two naval officers to assist you—Lieutenants Aschenfelter and O'Hearn—and that I was to replace Lieutenant O'Hearn. About the activities of the office I learned only that they include collection of some scientific and technical information."

Commander Rychly remained silent, so I continued.

"But I did get some advice from Mr. Jack Alberti in ONI."

Then, quietly, gently: "What did Jack Alberti say?"

"He was very complimentary to you; said I should keep my eyes and ears open and that I could learn a lot from you."

"That was good advice. I recommend that you follow it. We have many activities going on; many personalities, egos, and ambitions are involved, both American and German. You'll probably see and hear lots of things you don't understand. Just watch and listen for a few months and you'll figure it out. Keep an open mind—don't jump to conclusions. I have asked Lieutenant O'Hearn to brief you on his duties and introduce you to the others in the office. We'll talk again."

With that Commander Rychly stood up, indicating that our conversation was over. He walked me to the door of his office. Pointing across the foyer to the opposite office, he said, "That's LT Charlie O'Hearn's office, yours when he leaves in two weeks."

The telephone on Joe's desk rang. The call was for me from Lieutenant Aschenfelter, who welcomed me to Munich and invited me to dinner at his home that evening with his wife and the O'Hearns. He offered to pick me up at the hotel. Commander Rychly and Joe were watching as I gladly accepted.

4

THE PEOPLE OF POSSART PLATZ 3

The American Staff

Two navy officers—Charlie O'Hearn and Pete Aschenfelter—and three yeomen assisted the Skipper at Possart Platz 3. Joe Foster was the lead yeoman.

Late in the afternoon of my first day in Munich, LT Pete Aschenfelter greeted me as he opened the door of his late-model American car. Pete was a quiet sort. He said little and concentrated on his driving as the early evening darkness fell, but he did point out some landmarks we passed on our way. Especially impressive, in an unpleasant, foreboding way, were the high, gray, fortress-like walls of McGraw Kaserne, a former German Army facility, which after the war became the headquarters of the U.S. Seventh Army. The Kaserne's high and massive walls stretched for blocks along the Tegernseer Landstrasse, a major thoroughfare leading south from the city center. I passed those great walls many times in the succeeding months, and I shuddered each time. They rose above and dominated everything around them. Whether seen by daylight or by night through the glare of floodlights, their brutish strength seemed threatening, and notwithstanding their current use by the U.S. Army, they were to me a reminder of Hitler's Wehrmacht of World War II and of the death and destruction it wrought.

The Aschenfelters' house was one of the thousands of houses and apartments requisitioned by the U.S. Army for married officers and their families stationed in the American zone. The house, a comfortable middle-class German home, was on the Seyboldt Strasse in Harlaching, a section of Munich across the Isar River from and south of the city's center or "downtown."

LT Charlie O'Hearn and his wife, Ann, were already at the

Aschenfelters' house when I arrived. Pete's wife, Betsy, came downstairs; she had just fed their two girls and sent them upstairs to get ready for bed. The girls, however, were soon downstairs again, curious to see the grownups. Dinner was an informal occasion, with much talk of the pleasures and difficulties of life in Bavaria and the O'Hearns' plans for their fast approaching return to the States. While Pete said little, Charlie, a former Navy pilot grounded for reasons of health, was an outgoing, talkative Irishman. I liked my office colleagues and their wives. The evening was fun, but in compliance with security rules we did not talk about the office, and I learned nothing about my work.

The next morning Joe brought me again to Possart Platz 3. I went straight to Charlie O'Hearn's office. Charlie was seated behind a big desk in his bright and pleasant corner room. There was a window behind him and two large windows facing the snow-covered Possart Platz. Noticing that I was in uniform, Charlie told me that civilian dress was authorized and encouraged for officers except at certain times, which he would later explain.

The Skipper had asked him to brief me on his duties, for I was to assume them, but Charlie seemed uncomfortable, uncertain where to begin. Finally he took a stack of typewritten draft intelligence reports from his locked file cabinet and selected two to show me, one about a destroyer under construction at a shipyard in Poland and the other concerning a patent application filed at the German patent office in Munich for a new ship propeller design. The applicant was an engineer employed at an East German research institute. Handing me the reports, he said,

These are typical of the reports you will edit. The first is a report translated from German into English by our German intelligence staff here on this floor and the second is typical of some we receive in English draft from our German Science and Technology staff supervised by Pete Aschenfelter downstairs. You'll see hundreds, maybe thousands, of draft reports like these. Your job is to edit them for clarity and accuracy before approving them for final typing by our yeomen and submission up the chain of command to ONI. The bottom of each report contains space for comments about its significance, consistency with other information on hand, etc. Sometimes members of our German staff will add comments based on their experience and the extensive records they are keeping on subjects of interest. You may want to add comments of your own to any report if you think it will be helpful to the ONI analysts. But wait, you can start editing reports later; let me introduce you to our German staff.

The German Staff

The general intelligence group occupied three offices, separated from Charlie's corner office by a bathroom and a storage area stretching along the second floor corridor toward the back of the house. We stopped in each office in turn, meeting Karl Hetz, Max Parnitzki, and Helmuth Pich.

Karl Hetz, a stocky, blond man in his forties, jumped to his feet from his seat behind a desk as we arrived at his doorway and bid us to come in. Speaking English, Charlie introduced me as Lieutenant Junior Grade Durning, his just-arrived replacement. Drawing himself up at attention and almost clicking his heels, Hetz, with a nod of his head, said briskly, "I am pleased to meet you, Leutnant Durning." Our conversation was brief. My impression was that Mr. Hetz was quite formal and not fully fluent in spoken English. I learned from Charlie that Hetz was a former career officer of the German Navy, a *Fregaten Kapitän* (equivalent to a commander in the U.S. Navy) who had commanded a destroyer in the far northern waters of Norway during World War II. This first meeting with Hetz went reasonably well, but I was keenly aware that the difference in our ages—fifteen years or more—and Navy ranks could create problems if not handled with tact.

Maximilian Parnitzki was quite different from Hetz. In his thirties and speaking excellent English, Max was polite but less formal and more at ease. Replying to Charlie's statement that I was his replacement, Parnitzki gracefully said that he had enjoyed working with Lieutenant O'Hearn and wished him well in his next assignment. Then, turning to me with a smile, he said, "We do our best to provide you reports in good U.S. Navy English, but we still often make mistakes. We hope you will correct us so we may improve and make your work less burdensome."

His manner was professional yet friendly. I admired his style and felt he would be easy to work with. Later I learned that Max had been born and grew up in Kharkov, in the Soviet Union, where his father, a German engineer, was working for a German engineering firm. His mother was Russian. Max was bilingual in German and Russian, excellent in English, and managed well in Polish, too.

Finally, in the third office, Charlie introduced me to Helmuth Pich, a wiry man of medium height with a serious face and a military bearing. I guessed he was about forty years old. Like Karl Hetz, Pich was a former career naval officer. His manner was somewhat formal, but Pich's English was better than Hetz's. Pich was a Prussian who had grown up on one of the great Junker estates. He had entered the German Navy at a young age, became an officer, and served first as a naval aviator and then as a submarine commander in World War II. Helmuth Pich was tense throughout our brief conversation. I wondered if he ever relaxed.

To meet the S&T group we went downstairs to the first floor and into a large corner room—in the corner under Commander Rychly's office—with three desks and some tables. Charlie deferred to Pete Aschenfelter, who introduced me to the two translators who worked with him—Waldtraut Sellschopp and Toni Kinshofer. Both were young women in their twenties, graduates of German universities, with advanced study in languages. Both spoke and wrote excellent English. Fräulein Sellschopp, born and raised in North Germany—in Hamburg—had studied Russian as well as English. Fräulein Kinshofer was a native Bavarian, from Lenggries, a small town south of Munich.

Of the Science and Technology group I had only Dr. George Straimer left to meet. Dr. Straimer was not present that Monday morning. A few days later the Skipper called me to his office to meet Dr. Straimer. Dr. Straimer was a pleasant surprise; he was in his forties, dressed in a dark business suit, and had a large smile and a hearty handshake. He was at ease, joking with the Skipper, and without the customary German formality, he was soon joking with me about my need to learn *Bayerisch* (Bavarian dialect) to read menus, understand shopkeepers, and flirt with girls in Munich.

Dr. Straimer occupied a unique position at Possart Platz 3. He was assigned one of the diesel Mercedes cars, set his own schedule, and reported directly to the Skipper—privileges not afforded to the other German employees. Straimer was, according to the Skipper, an experienced physicist, who had headed a German research and development unit of the Luftwaffe working on *Funkbeobachtung* (radio intercepts and monitoring) during the war. At Possart Platz 3 he worked for the most part alone, coming and going as he determined. His office was on the first floor; it opened off the entrance hallway and, located at some considerable distance from the office of Pete Aschenfelter, Waldtraut Sellschopp, and Toni Kinshofer, was very private.

I soon came to know some of Dr. Straimer's work for Possart

Platz 3. The West German patent office was in the Deutsches Museum in Munich. Not only West German patent applications were filed there, however, for many persons or institutions in East Germany hoped for a reunification someday and sought patent protection for their inventions in both East and West. At regular intervals Dr. Straimer went to the patent office, taking Fräulein Sellschopp with him. Dr. Straimer reviewed all of the patent applications filed since his last visit and selected those of possible interest to the Navy. Fräulein Sellschopp made photocopies of the selected applications and took the copies back to the office where she and Fräulein Kinshofer translated them into English and put the translations into the standard form of Navy intelligence reports. Few dramatic new advances or breakthroughs were reported, but the steady stream of reports indicated the direction and progress of research in Germany on science and technology of interest to the Navy. The patent applications from East Germany were of interest not only for their scientific value but also because they indicated the subject matters and fields being pursued in the Soviet bloc, who was active in each field of research, and where each research facility was located.

Finally, and most important, Dr. Straimer was involved as an adviser to the leaders of the largest Bavarian political party, the Christian Social Union (CSU), which, together with its larger ally, Germany's Christian Democratic Union (CDU), controlled West Germany's *Bundestag* (parliament) in 1955 and 1956 and elected West Germany's president, Theodor Heuss, and its chancellor, Konrad Adenauer. Franz Josef Strauss, the CSU's leader, was a powerful member of the parliament of the Federal Republic. Adenauer made Strauss his minister of defense in 1956, and Dr. Straimer, a close friend and supporter of Strauss, came to hold high offices in the scientific and technical field in the Adenauer government.

There were other stories about Dr. Straimer. The Skipper told me of a youthful prank that could have put Straimer in serious trouble. Straimer was a student at Munich's Technische Hochschule when Hitler came to speak there. With some fellow students, he adjusted the microphone sound system to eliminate all the lower frequencies. As a result, Hitler's voice was heard as a high-pitched squeak, which caused laughter in the audience. Hitler did not find the joke funny, and Straimer might have had a significant problem had other matters not diverted the Führer's attention. Years later Dr. Straimer went into a Luftwaffe research unit conducting high-priority work and stayed there throughout the war. Fortunately he suffered no consequences because of the prank.

Many former German soldiers and seamen had memorable stories of their surrender, but none surpassed Dr. Straimer's. With a slight smile he described how his research unit fled from Berlin in a convoy of trucks as the Russian Army approached from the east. They headed south toward Bavaria but were forced to stop frequently to make way for tanks, armored vehicles, and thousands of soldiers and refugees crowding the roads. It took several days but they finally arrived at a place to rest, a large farmhouse fifteen or twenty miles northwest of Munich. The farmhouse had a yard large enough for the trucks and a farmer kind enough to let Straimer and his colleagues share his house.

Straimer and the members of his unit knew that the American army was advancing into Bavaria and that they would probably have to surrender themselves before long. They wanted, however, to surrender with dignity. The morning after their arrival at the farmhouse they took advantage of the chance to wash themselves and their clothing and hung their clothes out to dry in the sun. They themselves, clad in their underwear, started to cook the only food they could find in the house, several large heads of cabbage.

Later that morning they were surprised to hear noises of heavy vehicles approaching. Several American tanks rolled into the farmyard followed by truckloads of American soldiers. The Germans had no choice; they had to raise their hands and surrender. As Dr. Straimer said, "It is difficult to present an appearance of dignity while standing in a farmhouse kitchen in your underwear with the smell of cabbage in the background."

Possart Platz 3 was run in first-class style. In addition to the six U.S. Navy personnel and the six German professional staff were four others important to the operation of the house and grounds: Herr Schnabel, a retired Munich police officer, served as guard and doorman; Frau Raab, the *Putzfrau* (cleaning woman), a round, good-natured and motherly Bavarian woman, kept the office spotlessly clean and put on a white uniform to bring coffee or tea mid morning and mid-afternoon to all who wanted it; Herr Staudinger, the *Hausmeister*, served as a janitor, manager of household utilities, car washer, and jack-of-all-trades; and Frau Staudinger assisted her husband and made extra money by doing laundry for the U.S. Navy officers and enlisted personnel. The Staudingers were a lovely, working-class Bavarian couple who were always smiling and willing to help.

Security

The premises were secure. Someone was present at the house at all times. The three sailors—yeomen—were quartered in a suite of rooms with a bathroom on the third floor of the house. Each had a separate room, luxurious in comparison with the usual Navy barracks or shipboard quarters. The Staudingers lived in a small house on the grounds in back of the main house. All entrance doors and windows had locks.

By day Herr Schnabel sat in the reception area guarding entry through the main door and access to the stairway. No one except U.S. and German staff was allowed beyond the reception area without authorization of one of the American Navy officers. By night the house was locked and one or more of the enlisted personnel, as well as the Staudingers, were present. The sailors rotated the duty of standing watch in the house from the end of the workday to the office opening in the morning. In accordance with Navy security rules, no unauthorized personnel were allowed in the house at any time. All classified papers were locked in appropriate cabinets or safes when not in use. All U.S. personnel were briefed on the security rules. In addition to telephones at all working desks, a state-of-the-art intercom system connected the Skipper's office, my office, the yeomen's desks, and the yeomen's third-floor quarters.

But no security system is perfect, and it can be penetrated when the will to do so is strong. One Sunday morning I came into the office to do some work. As I sat down I heard voices, a man's voice and a woman's. It took me a moment or so to recognize that the sleepy voices were coming in on our intercom system. After another few seconds I understood that the voices were coming from the yeomen's quarters on the third floor. The sailor speaking was a recent arrival to our office; I had briefed him myself on the security rules. I spoke into the intercom, identified myself, and ordered the sailor to get dressed, remove his guest from the house, and then report to me with her name and address. He responded, "Aye, aye, sir," in a frightened voice. I then telephoned the Skipper at his home. We agreed that this yeoman was not suitable for our office. The next morning the Skipper called COMNAVGER, and by noon the sailor had transfer orders and was on a train back to COMNAVGER in Heidelberg.

5

"ANOTHER INTELLIGENCE ORGANIZATION"

By my second week in Munich I was feeling pretty good about my assignment. I was editing reports more quickly and with more confidence in the results, as I learned to discuss awkward or ambiguous translations with the authors, that is, with Messrs. Hetz, Parnitzki, and Pich. More came from Max Parnitzki and Helmuth Pich than from Karl Hetz, and I wondered what else he might be doing, but rather than ask, I decided to watch, listen, and keep an open mind.

On Tuesday of his last week, O'Hearn told me to come to work the next day in uniform, as he would introduce me to another part of my duties, a part best done in uniform. He was quite secretive regarding this responsibility, lowering his voice to say, "You will replace me as liaison to the Navy section of another intelligence organization. Tomorrow afternoon we'll go there and I'll introduce you. They are all former German Navy officers. They speak excellent English. They are expecting us. I will tell you more tomorrow as we drive there."

The tingly feeling came again. I wanted to know more but asked no questions. I heard the voice of Jack Alberti: "Keep your eyes open and listen carefully . . . "

The next morning was a long one, but at last, in mid-afternoon, we left in Charlie's assigned car. "We are going to Pullach, a village just beyond the southern edge of Munich, across the Isar River. I'll mark the way on a map, but you'll also have to watch for landmarks for there are many turns, many places to get lost."

The way from Bogenhausen to Pullach was indeed long and confusing and meandered across almost the whole city. Charlie chose, and I also later followed, a route southward along the Tegernseer Landstrasse and past McGraw Kaserne.

After all these years, I still remember the way—from the Tegernseer

Landstrasse a right turn (westward) onto the Nauplia Strasse, which bent slightly and changed its name to the Seyboldt Strasse in Harlaching. From the Seyboldt to the Grünwalder Strasse and down into the valley of the Isar, across a bridge over the river, up out of the valley, and a left turn to Pullach and to the street leading to our destination.

Charlie's briefing was not extensive. He told me only that we were going to the Navy section of a super secret German intelligence organization, "the Gehlen Organization," a large intelligence collection and evaluation undertaking directed at the Soviet bloc. My role, Charlie said, was liaison at the Navy evaluation section; I would provide support as requested, usually in the form of copies of unclassified technical U.S. Navy publications. "Arrangements have been made for you to replace me," Charlie said, "and you will want to visit the Navy section regularly—I go weekly, on Wednesday afternoons—and on such other occasions as you think useful. I recommend that you work out your schedule with them and also call in advance each time to be sure they know you are coming and to inform the guards at the gate. I'll give you the telephone number back at the office."

We arrived at the gate, showed our U.S. Navy identification cards to one of the two uniformed armed guards, who after examining them closely, comparing the photos with our own faces, handed them back, snapped to attention, and crisply said, "Bitte, passen Sie herein" (Please come in).

The organization was housed in an extensive walled compound, a small town or campus unto itself, with a grid pattern of streets, one large and elegant house, and a whole town of separate smaller houses. The grounds were pleasant and park like, with many trees, covered by snow in the winter and green like a Bavarian forest in summer. Charlie drove us to the house containing on its ground floor the offices of the Navy Evaluation Section, parked along the curb, and led me to the door of the house. The door opened quickly and a smiling man in his sixties greeted us, "Guten Tag! Wir haben das Auto durch den Fenster schon gesehen [Good day! We saw the car through the window]. Oh, excuse me, I should practice my English. Please, come in."

Herr Wilhelm Hadeler was his name. He took us into a large room with desks along the walls. Several people came forward to meet us. They all seemed quite relaxed and friendly. The leader was a tall blond man in his forties, Herr Albrecht Obermaier, called "Sepp." He introduced himself and then the others, Herr Alfred Schulze-Hinrichs, Herr Hadeler, Herr Helmut Möhlmann, and the group's attractive young secretary and general office manager, Fräulein Anni von Trotha. The men were clearly fond of Miss von Trotha, whom they called "Trautchen." She was from a famous German Navy family, a descendent of Admiral Adolf von Trotha who served in the highest ranks of the Kaiser's navy along with leaders such as Admirals Alfred von Tirpitz and Reinhard Scheer.

We were invited to take coffee with the section. They pulled up chairs for all to be seated at a table, calling it "the officers' mess." We talked for quite a while about the usual topics discussed when people meet—where each was born, where educated, service in our respective navies, and so on. Since I was much younger than the Germans (except Trautchen) and of considerably lower naval rank, I was careful to address them with respect. Nothing of substance was discussed, and our meeting ended with their expressions of their good wishes to Charlie on his departure and their welcome to me. "All in all, a good— or at least a friendly—start," I thought, "but I didn't learn much about them, or what I am supposed to do." Charlie offered no more information, so I asked. "What is this organization? What does it do? Who runs it? What does the U.S. Navy have to do with it? What am I supposed to do?"

"Good questions. Ask Rychly," came the reply—and that was all.

During the months that followed, I came to feel comfortable with the members of "the officers' mess." I felt accepted when I, along with the Skipper, was invited to a cocktail party at the home of Herr Schulze-Hinrichs. Later I was invited to a large Gehlen Organization Christmas party of a hundred or more people at a hall in the compound. I was seated next to Trautchen at the Navy Evaluation Section's table. Both occasions were warm and friendly.

Suspicions

Charlie O'Hearn was about to leave for his new duty station in New York City. Pete Aschenfelter was a quiet man who kept to himself. He arrived on time at 8:00 a.m., worked away all day and left promptly at 4:00 p.m. The few times we talked I learned little about him. Neither Charlie nor Pete socialized with the German professional staff. They were both married, and the Aschenfelters had two small children. They appeared to live within the American military community in Harlaching and Perlacher Forst. Both were quite cordial to me in the office, but after my first meal at the Aschenfelters, at the time of my arrival, I was not invited again. Charlie and Pete acted at times as if there were two teams in the office—themselves on one and the Skipper and "the Germans" on the other. I suppose I was still so new that they never decided to which team I belonged. Charlie left first, but Pete received his orders for transfer shortly thereafter. Then the Skipper and I were alone, together with the German staff, of course.

On the morning of O'Hearn's last day, he and I were in his (soon to be my) office. He had already turned over his desk, chair, and responsibilities to me. We were about to go downstairs to his assigned Mercedes, where he would show me the tricks of starting the diesel engine, letting it warm up, etc., and then he would turn over the keys to me. Pete Aschenfelter came upstairs carrying some reports for me to edit and joined our conversation about the car.

Suddenly we heard a commotion downstairs. The voice of a woman talking loudly, excitedly, almost angrily, in German was reverberating up the atrium to us, followed by the Skipper's husky voice trying to calm her. There were footsteps on the staircase as the Skipper and the woman climbed to the second floor. Through my own open doorway I saw a well-dressed elderly German woman in her sixties follow the Skipper into his office, complaining all the way about his failure to give her adequate notice and her need to shop immediately for the ingredients for a dinner for ten people that evening. The door to his office closed and we could hear no more.

Curiosity overcame me. "Who was that?" I asked.

"That was Frau Mattheus, or Mrs. Matthews if you prefer, Commander Rychly's so-called housekeeper," said Charlie. "She comes in from time to time. They supposedly go shopping together. She always seems to be complaining about something or other. I don't trust her, and I don't see why he doesn't get rid of her. There must be something going on."

"Careful, Charlie," said Pete holding his finger to his lips, "not here."

Charlie, now with the bravery of a short timer, lowered his voice almost to a whisper and, turning to me, said, "Be careful, Marvin. Pete is right. Rychly has this whole house bugged . . . and the telephones, too." Pete said nothing, but nodded his head in agreement.

I was stunned.

6

A HIGHLY PRODUCTIVE
INTELLIGENCE OFFICE

Many months passed before another officer arrived. Consequently, I was the only Navy officer present to work with
Commander Rychly for most of my time in Munich. I was fortunate,
for I was quickly given more responsibilities, more opportunities to
assist in his projects, more occasions to watch, listen, and learn. The
Skipper and I grew closer as the days, weeks, and months rolled by.

Volume and Range of Reports

I worked long hours to keep up with the flow of reports that crossed
my desk, but I also learned a great deal from them. I became familiar
with the geography of the North Sea, the Baltic (*Ostsee*), the Barents
Sea, and the White Sea, and familiar with port facilities in Travemünde,
Rostock, Stralsund, Rügen, Peenemünde, Swinemünde, Stettin,
Gdansk, Riga, Tallinn, Leningrad, Archangel, and Murmansk. Often
information about the ports included photos of the fortifications,
cargo-handling facilities, dry-docks, and ship construction. All of the
Soviet bloc ports in the Baltic, large and small—all of the ports from
Travemünde to Leningrad—were covered, and I edited similar reports
about Murmansk on the Barents Sea and Archangel on the White Sea.

I learned the characteristics of Soviet and Polish warships of various sizes and classes, the daily time schedule of the ship's activities,
the training of personnel, and even the nutritional value of the Soviet
and Polish crews' standard rations. I saw photos of Soviet warships
and of the small coastal vessels of the East German border police.
There were reports of the underwater sound characteristics of Soviet
and Polish warships, including submarines. These "sound prints" were
the products of somebody's hydrophones or other listening devices in
the Baltic Sea or the Kattegat and Skagerak, which form the narrow

exit from the Baltic to the North Sea and thence to the Atlantic.

Similarly, I saw reports of Danube river traffic—boats, barges, cargos, piers, docks, and cranes—all the way from Passau at the border of Germany and Austria through the Balkans to the mouth of the Danube at Constanta on the Black Sea. I had to conclude that the organization supplying these reports was a large one, that it had agents aboard numerous ships and boats, at sea and on the Danube, and perhaps had agents in the ports as well.

I also became familiar with the reports of patent applications coming to me in English from our S&T section (translations by Waldtraut Sellschopp and Toni Kinshofer). These reports were sometimes a source of frustration and humor for the translators and for me, for their descriptions of mechanical devices were of little meaning to us. They frequently described a diagram full of arrows, circles, triangles with wording like this: "Number 1 pushes against number 2, which turns number 3 and engages with number 4 . . . " The descriptions were clear in one sense but left us with little understanding of what the device did and how it was to be used. Nevertheless, ONI's S&T section liked the reports.

All in all the number of reports that crossed my desk was great and was increasing. I remembered the comment by Lieutenant Junior Grade Christianson in Berlin that there were too many reports from Munich, more than the small staff could generate. His instincts were right, of course, but at that time, on the American side, only the Skipper, the DNI in Washington, and a handful of persons in the Central Intelligence Agency (CIA) knew what was going on.

I strongly suspected that the reports, which came to us in German, were from the Gehlen Organization, from the operations, that is, collection, branch of the organization, but not from the evaluation and analysis office that I visited regularly in my capacity as liaison officer. It did not surprise me that Lieutenant Junior Grade Christianson appeared to be unaware of the existence of the Gehlen Organization, for most Germans, like most Americans, had never heard of it, or if they had heard of it, they knew little or nothing about it.

Some of the reports raised enough questions in my mind that I discussed them with the Skipper. For example, in addition to the reports on ports, ships, and naval personnel, we received a steady stream of reports about the movements and the cargo of trains in East Germany. Sometimes we received as many as a dozen rail traffic reports at a time. One morning I brought the Skipper a pile of edited rail traffic reports to sign. I commented that I found very little in the contents of any single report to be of interest to the Navy but that it was very interesting that, taken together, they covered train movements all over East Germany, often included statistics of total movements and cargo, and arrived at our office with little delay.

"And what does that tell you about the source of the reports?" the Skipper asked.

"That the information comes from multiple observers, probably workers at the stations or on the trains, or, in the case of the statistics, from an administrative office of the East German railroad system, and that the intelligence organization collecting the information has an effective way to get the reports quickly to the West," I replied.

"Yes, and it's a large net familiar with railroad matters, whose existence raises opportunities to accomplish other tasks—like contact with other railroad men on trains with which they connect, such as railroad workers in Poland and Czechoslovakia, and through them possibly with railroad workers in other parts of the Eastern bloc. The Gehlen Organization is good at collection in East Germany, but it gets more difficult as you go farther east. Tracking railway movements is a classic intelligence activity used to determine enemy intentions. Any increase in movements of Soviet bloc military forces, equipment, or supplies toward the West or to the Soviet Army bases in East Germany could signal coming trouble.

"Those reports aren't individually of much specific interest to the Navy, but I've watched the net grow over the last few years and have seen the reports improve. The Russians can't move a rail car in East Germany without our knowing about it soon after the move. And that's not all—those reports, taken together, form a picture of an important Gehlen Organization activity, monitoring rail transport for indications of a Russian build up. Watching the flow of reports is a way to watch the Gehlen Organization as well as the Soviets."

My mind fixed on the words "Gehlen Organization"—because they confirmed my suspicions about the source of the reports I edited—and "watch the Gehlen Organization's activities." Was that part of our mission? What, if anything, was I supposed to accomplish by my visits to Gehlen's Navy Evaluation Section?

I didn't have to ask; the Skipper read my mind and continued, "Our role here is complicated. The Federal Republic is our ally and our mission is intelligence about the Soviet bloc, but we can't close our eyes to all things we learn about our German partner."

"And what am I supposed to do in my contacts with Gehlen's Navy section?"

"Nothing for now. You are new to the scene. You are getting along fine. Just keep your eyes and ears open. Get to know your German colleagues. Get involved in their lives, as a friend. Take your time; each person is unique. Watch long enough and you will understand what motivates each person. Is it money? Love? Sex? Power? Recognition? We'll talk more about this later."

At first I received for editing only reports already translated into English by our own German staff. After a month or so, however, I began receiving piles of reports in German with the request that I pass them to the German staff for translation. They were brought to me by Joe, our yeoman first class, but they came from the Skipper himself. Finally one day, about a month or so after my arrival, the Skipper walked into my office and put a pile of German language reports on my desk, saying, "Please have these translated and prepared for submission to ONI via Captain Day in Berlin. Please scan the reports in German before distributing them for translation. If you see anything special or urgent or otherwise unusual, bring it to my attention at once."

The Skipper did not say how these reports came to be in his hands. Naturally, I was curious—indeed, keenly interested—but I remembered Jack Alberti's advice, so I did not ask. I was pleased, however, that the Skipper's confidence in me was clearly growing.

Interrogations

In the early years after the opening of the Munich office in 1948, a substantial part of the office's workload was the interrogation of people living in the many refugee or displaced person camps in the vicinity of Munich. Some of these people had information of interest to the Navy. This had changed, however, by the time I arrived in early 1955. Hundreds of thousands of displaced persons had passed through the camps and found new lives in West Germany or by emigration abroad. While I was in Munich we conducted only a few interrogations; I was involved with two, and I remember them well.

One morning in the spring of 1955 the Skipper came into my office quite early, closed the door and said, "The Army says it has a Polish defector who may be of interest to us. He is a Polish merchant marine officer who jumped ship in a north German port. The Army has him in a safe house in Munich but will bring him to one of its interrogation rooms at an Army facility at an agreed time. I'd like you to go with Max, see what it is all about, and size up the source. Max will speak Polish with him and will keep the questions general until we see whether the source will talk with us, whether he knows anything of interest to us, and whether we can believe him. Max will tell you the gist of the conversation in English. You and Max will report your impressions to me.

"And one more thing—put on your uniform and carry your Navy ID. You are there to deal with the Army and to reassure the Polish defector that he really is talking with the U.S. Navy. Watch how Max approaches the situation. Max is a good interrogator, so you'll learn. Watch the source also for any signs of emotions, including body language. Here is the name and phone number of the Army officer in charge. Check with Max before setting the time, but try to go today."

"Aye-aye, Sir" seemed appropriate, so I said it; the Skipper smiled and said, "Carry on."

I called the Army officer in charge and agreed on a meeting with the defector at 2:00 p.m. in an Army building near Munich's *Ostbahnhof* (East train station). He gave me the address and a description of the building. Changing into uniform was easy, for my apartment was only a few blocks away in the Schumann Strasse. I was excited at the prospect of taking part in an interrogation and pleased that the Skipper had enough confidence in me to assign me this duty.

I drove and Max guided me directly to the Ostbahnhof and then to the nearby address which, we discovered, was in a warehouse district. The Army's building was a one-story gray concrete structure that was identical to the warehouse buildings around it. The only entrance had a small placard beside the door that read, "U.S. Army— *Kein Eintritt*" (No Entry), a doorbell, and a small microphone.

I pushed the bell and a voice with an unmistakable Brooklyn accent said, "State your name, rank, unit, and nature of your business here."

"Lieutenant JG Marvin Durning, U.S. Navy, Munich office of Commander Naval Forces, Germany, to meet with Captain Foley [not his real name] at 1400 hours. With me is Mr. Max Parnitzki, a German citizen and member of the staff of our office. Our business is classified, but is known to Captain Foley."

"Just a minute, Lieutenant," came the reply; then, after a short wait, "When you hear a buzz, turn the handle of the door and enter. Show your ID and sign in at the guard desk just inside the door."

We followed the directions and a soldier escorted us to the office of Captain Foley, who greeted us warmly, gave us coffee, and described the defector: he was thirty-three years old, a career officer of the Polish merchant marine, with a rank equivalent to a first officer, i.e., the next in command after a merchant ship captain. After a few minutes Captain Foley called in a sergeant who escorted us down a long corridor with soldiers working at desks on either side until we came to a plain door that opened into a windowless room in which the only furniture was a large table and some chairs. Standing beside the table was the Polish merchant marine officer dressed in his dark blue uniform. He was smoking a cigarette; his face was flushed; his eyes were red as if he had not slept. He was obviously very nervous. The sergeant said something to him in Polish and told him we were representatives of the U.S. Navy who wanted to talk with him. He said nothing but looked nervously at me and at Max. Finally, Max spoke to him in Polish and received a curt reply.

"He wants to see proof that we are from the U.S. Navy," Max said to me.

I pulled out my wallet and showed the Pole my Navy ID card. Max showed his ID and a letter stating that he was employed by U.S. Naval Forces, Germany, in its Munich office. The Pole looked at our cards and letter but obviously could not read the English. He looked at us intently and nervously but said nothing. He had smoked his cigarette down to the butt, so Max offered him another and held out his lighter. The Pole, still very tense, took the cigarette, lighted it, and drew deeply on it. Then he took from inside his coat pocket a crumpled envelope with a letter inside. It was addressed to him from someone in Cleveland, Ohio. He showed it to each of us in turn but would not let us hold it. All the while he spoke excitedly in Polish and said over and over a word I recognized as "Cleveland."

Max translated: "He says he has an uncle in Cleveland and the letter invites him to come to Cleveland. That's all he will say until we arrange for him to go to his uncle in Cleveland, with all necessary papers and transportation. He is so worked up, so tense, and so afraid that we will send him back to Poland that he looks as if he is going to break down. We can't interrogate him while he is in this condition. I recommend that I tell him that we can't help him get to Cleveland unless he cooperates with us, so he should get a hold of himself and think it over. We would see him again in a day or two and hope to be able to help him."

I agreed with Max's recommendation, left the room, found the sergeant at a nearby desk, and explained our decision and hope to see the Polish officer again in the next day or so, after he had had some sleep and got hold of himself. The sergeant thought that a good idea and said he would explain to Captain Foley, who had left for the day. I rejoined Max and the Pole and found the Pole even more tense and red in the face, saying "Cleveland" over and over again. The Sergeant took the Polish officer out of the room. Max and I signed out, left the building, and drove back to Possart Platz 3.

I called Captain Foley the next morning—a Friday—to make another appointment and was told that the Polish officer was still very tense and frightened and did not feel well. Captain Foley thought we should wait until Monday. On Monday morning I called again, only to receive a shock. The Polish officer had suffered a massive stroke and was in the Army hospital in critical condition. I called again early Tuesday morning and was told that the Polish officer had died of his stroke. I wondered whether anyone would advise his uncle in Cleveland. I never found out.

My second interrogation experience came a month or so later and was not nearly so dramatic. Again the Skipper gave me instructions about a border crosser, an engineer, who appeared to be of interest to the Navy. Again I was to go with Max to accomplish an interrogation of the engineer, who had been employed in an East German research institute until his recent escape to West Germany. He was not in the Army's hands; he was instead staying with friends in a town near Munich while obtaining necessary papers from the West German authorities and looking for employment. Max and I went to the town and to his address. We knocked on the door of a small, well-kept house with a garden in front. A woman came to the door, and in reply to Max's request to see Herr Ingenieur Schmidt (not his real name), she asked who we were and why we wanted to see Herr Schmidt. Max explained that we were with the U.S. Navy and that we did not seek to do Schmidt any harm, but rather we wanted to learn from him information that could be helpful to both the United States and Germany in the years ahead. To our great relief, she invited us into her living room and called to the engineer to come down from the second floor to meet us.

After some introductory small talk, Max began asking easy questions about the engineer's birth date and place, his early school years, higher education, and so on, and gradually came to his employment at the naval research institute. Max was so nonthreatening, indeed so respectful and reassuring, that the engineer spoke freely of the institute's research projects, the successes and failures to date, and the specialized fields of each of his former colleagues. We could not have wished for better cooperation. He asked only that we not make public his name or presence in Munich—for after all, the borders of the DDR and of Communist Czechoslovakia were only a short distance away. We gave him that assurance, and I continue to keep my promise in these pages written fifty years after the interrogation.

I was pleased with my progress so far, and amazed at all that the Skipper had accomplished in the years since he first established the intelligence office at Possart Platz 3. He had recruited an outstanding team of German personnel and organized for the receipt of intelligence from the Gehlen Organization. The office was highly productive, and I felt good about its operation and my role in it. I thought I knew what was going on.

7

U.S. NAVY VISITORS

This productive but mysterious office in Munich attracted important U.S. Navy visitors, both during my one-year tenure there and before. Our Navy visitors included the director of naval intelligence (DNI) from Washington, D.C.; the newly designated naval attaché to the U.S. embassy in Moscow, en route to his post; and, most memorable of all, Undersecretary of the Navy Thomas L. Gates. Commander Rychly asked my assistance as driver in all of these visits, but I was not present at his closed-door discussions with the DNI or with the Moscow naval attaché. This didn't bother me; I had no need to know.

Undersecretary Gates's visit to Munich was both memorable and enjoyable. It occurred in the early summer of 1955 and was, in military fashion, preceded by sixty or ninety days of intense planning, speculation, and signals traffic among the Office of the Undersecretary in the Pentagon, the Commander-in-Chief Naval Forces Northeast Atlantic and Mediterranean (CINCNELM) in London, the Commander Naval Forces, Germany (COMNAVGER), the Commander of the U.S. Seventh Army in McGraw Kaserne in Munich, and various other Army and State Department offices. There was a storm of messages, especially between the Seventh Army and Army headquarters in the Pentagon, with copies to everyone including us.

The first message from the Pentagon announced a trip by the undersecretary to Europe for a series of meetings, with a one-weekend break to relax in Munich and its surroundings. The undersecretary asked that there be no formalities or meetings during his weekend visit; he wished to arrive quietly and inconspicuously and attract no attention to himself or his party while he was in town. Those instructions raised a challenge for the Seventh Army, the major military command of Bavaria, for it was determined to provide a reception worthy of an undersecretary and to assign enough manpower to anticipate and fulfill the undersecretary's every wish.

The Skipper, our three yeomen, and I constituted the total U.S. Navy presence in Bavaria. We were directed by COMNAVGER in Heidelberg to render any assistance the undersecretary might request and were left on our own to work out the details. As we understood the situation, Undersecretary Gates would be traveling in a Navy plane and was to be quietly and informally met and assisted in Bavaria by us.

The undersecretary was to arrive in the morning at München-Riem, Munich's civilian airport. I kept the Skipper informed of the Army signal traffic, which was filled with suggestions for "courtesies" to be rendered by the Army to Mr. Gates and his party. The Skipper and I decided that we should not try to match the Army but should honor the undersecretary's wishes for a quiet and inconspicuous time of relaxation. We decided to take two of our old Mercedes diesels to the airport (one driven by each of us) in case his party was larger than could fit comfortably in one car. Our faithful chief yeoman, Joe, would follow in our Navy pickup to carry luggage.

The day of the arrival dawned bright and sunny. We met at the office and drove in a column of three vehicles to the airport. As we approached the airport entrance we were surprised and amused to see a long convoy of Army cars and trucks stretching from the airport entrance road, past the terminal, and out onto the tarmac. What looked like a battalion of military police covered the airport and its parking lots. We drove to a gate, showed our credentials to an Army guard, and were allowed to drive onto the tarmac to the area in front of the terminal where the Army had established an honor guard in full dress uniform to greet the undersecretary, including a soldier bearing the American flag. We could only smile at the Army's interpretation of a quiet and inconspicuous arrival.

The irony was heightened, moreover, by the spectacle of the arrival of the undersecretary's plane. It was a large, four-engine plane, painted gleaming white with "U.S. Navy" in dark blue on its side. The most dramatic feature, however, was the four propellers, painted in red, white, and blue stripes, which formed red, white, and blue bulls-eye patterns as the propellers turned. The plane landed and taxied toward us. It was a beautiful sight, a giant red, white, and blue bird rolling toward us and the glass-walled terminal building behind us—just the way to enter a small German civilian airport "quietly and inconspicuously."

I glanced behind me and saw dozens of passengers and airport staff looking at us through the glass wall of the terminal, and German airport police in groups staring at the scene.

The plane stopped and stairs were rolled out to it. A group of Army officers, led by a colonel in full dress, moved forward to the foot of the stairs. The Skipper and I took our places at the foot of the stairs on the other side. The plane's engines stopped and its exit door swung open. A tall man in his forties—the undersecretary—started through the door but stopped as he saw the array of Army officers, the honor guard, and the convoy of Army vehicles. I heard him distinctly—he said, "Aw, shit," and went back into the plane. A few moments later, his naval aide, a full captain in uniform with aiguillette and medals, came down the steps and spoke briefly with the Army colonel and his entourage of officers, thanking them for the reception. He then turned to us, and we identified ourselves as Navy representatives of COMNAVGER, present to assist the undersecretary. The aide re-entered the plane and soon came back accompanied by the undersecretary, who briefly thanked the Army group, turned to us, and after introductions said, "Let's get out of here before the mayor, the whole city council, and a swarm of reporters arrive."

Joe put their luggage in the pickup. The Skipper, Mr. Gates, and his naval aide led the way in the first car. I followed in our second car and Joe followed me. It was a short drive from the airport to Bogenhausen and to Possart Platz 3, where we went to the Skipper's office to discuss what they would like to see and do. They relaxed and accepted our suggestion of a brief tour of Munich, a visit to a typical Bavarian beer hall, and some dinner. The next day they spent in Garmisch-Partenkirchen and its surrounding areas, and then they went back to their schedule of meetings.

The tour of Munich went well, but the beer hall was the hit of the day. Both Mr. Gates and his aide were warm and informal people, interested in things typical of Bavaria. Taking them at their word, we took them to the Hofbräuhaus and indeed into *die Schwemme*—a large, noisy, ground floor beer hall where German workers and American soldiers on leave filled the large tables, drinking one-liter steins of beer, with pretzels and giant "beer radishes" (*Bierrettich*). A beer radish is huge; it can be as much as 12 inches long. It is cut round and round in a spiral shape and doused with salt. When the salt has drawn water from all over the radish it is ready to be eaten, but patience is important—you must wait "*bis er weint*" (until it cries).

Everything was served by stout Bavarian waitresses wearing dirndls, while an "oom-pah-pah" brass band pounded out Bavarian beer-drinking songs, including "*In München steht ein Hofbräuhaus*" (In Munich stands a Hofbräuhaus) and "*I mög gern a bier seh', so gross wie der Schliersee*" (in Bavarian dialect, "I want a beer, as big as Lake Schlier"), and ended each set with "*ein Prosit der Gemütlichkeit*" (a toast to Gemütlichkeit [see the glossary]). *Die Schwemme* is a distinctly lowbrow place. The crowd is noisy and enthusiastic, the music is simple and loud, the beer is cold and good. Mr. Gates and his aide joined in the spirit of large beers, songs familiar to Bavarians, and loud music. We all enjoyed ourselves immensely.

Some weeks later the Skipper received a letter from the undersecretary thanking both of us for our help in making his visit a pleasure. A copy of that letter is Appendix D.

PART 2

LIFE IN MUNICH

8

GERMAN FRIENDS MADE: MAX'S PARTY

My first months in Munich went well outside the office as well as in. I especially remember the first few weeks. In addition to becoming familiar with my job, I learned my way from the hotel to the office, obtained a U.S. forces driver's license, and celebrated the arrival of the trunk carrying my clothes and books.

First Friends

On Saturday of my first weekend I explored Munich, started a review of German with my college textbook, and continued my reading of German history. I also discovered that I liked Bavarian food, especially *Leberknödelsuppe* (liver dumpling soup) as served in the Rathauskeller (the restaurant in the basement of the city hall) by a pretty young waitress named Erni. Erni guided me through the menu, and I went back to the Rathauskeller frequently during the next year.

Sunday that weekend was a cold, gray day. There were only a few guests in the hotel, and I ate breakfast alone in a mostly empty dining room. I read the Army newspaper in five minutes and wondered what to do next. I walked in the vicinity of the hotel, past shuttered shops and empty buildings, but the brisk wind, icy streets, and absence of people made walking uncomfortable and depressing. In Germany all shops closed on Sundays, and there was little to do. Cold and bored, I returned to the hotel.

Entering the warm but empty lobby, I was greeted by sounds of young girls' laughter and saw three adolescent girls surrounding the friendly blond German woman who, on duty behind the hotel's reception desk, had greeted me on my arrival. Seeing me, she hushed her girls, smiled, and made me welcome by her Bavarian greeting, "Grüss Gott, Leutnant Durning." Switching to her accented English,

59

she introduced her happy group: "I am Gertrude Stilgenbauer and these are my daughters Renate, Irmi, and Elli. They are out of school for the weekend." The girls all smiled and I found myself smiling back, charmed by the warm and bright happiness of the four of them on this cold, dark, depressing winter day.

Gertrude was a cheerful, warmhearted person, and soon she was asking me where I was from and whether I was staying in Munich or passing through. In answering, I tried to practice my German. Gertrude and her girls were delighted, supplied needed words at critical points, and gently corrected my mistakes. I learned that Renate was sixteen years old; Irmi, almost fourteen; and Elli, twelve.

Gertrude explained that she lived in a room on the top floor of the hotel as part of her job, and the girls lived at a Catholic convent school, which they could leave only on designated weekends. She had been looking for an apartment for many months, but housing was very scarce in Munich and mostly too expensive. They all crowded into her one room on weekends like this. She was grateful to have even one room and to know that her girls were safe at their school. I wondered why she did not mention her husband but thought it better not to ask.

Gertrude invited me to have tea with them that afternoon, when she was finished with work. Several hours later, I was seated on a chair in her room with the four of them, speaking German better and better, and having a fine time—I had been adopted as a friend. I saw Gertrude and the girls from time to time during my stay in Munich and through them learned something of the difficulties of everyday life for most Germans in Bavaria.

Housing

I had much to do to settle in. Normally the Seventh Army housing office would assign me a room in its Bachelor Officers Quarters (BOQ) in McGraw Kaserne, but the Skipper knew how the Army housing system worked. He wrote a letter to the American Army officer in charge of the housing office stating that my duties required that I be housed outside the Kaserne (or any other U.S. facility), in housing where I could have unrestricted contact with the city's German, indeed international, population. He knew, of course, that the Army had many requisitioned apartments and houses in Munich's residential neighborhoods.

A young German woman from the housing office took me on a tour of available units. Luck was with me. I was shown and immediately accepted a fully equipped and furnished two-bedroom apartment in a pleasant building, with private off-street parking, at 11 Schu-mann Strasse in Bogenhausen, only a few blocks from Possart Platz. She warned me, however, that more new apartment buildings for American personnel were under construction at Perlacher Forst, an area set aside for the American forces in Munich, and all requisitioned apartments would be returned to their German owners in a few months. Consequently, I would have to move out of my apartment in the near future.

The Army treated me well. In addition to the fully equipped apartment, parking, telephone, and other utilities, it provided a register of household personnel who had been cleared by the Army and German police with respect to security, crime, and health and were subject to periodic review of these factors in order to maintain their clearance. The woman who showed me the apartment recommended a cleaning woman from the register, Frau Schiller (not her real name), who had worked for the apartment's prior occupants. I gladly hired her to come regularly to clean the apartment. The first day she came early in the morning. When we met, Frau Schiller assured me that she understood my wishes and would bring *Alles in Ordnung* (everything in order). And thus I was spoiled for several months by a motherly woman in her fifties or sixties who rode her bicycle to the job, washed dirty dishes, scrubbed everything until it shined, changed the linens every week, and placed on my bed a neatly folded pair of clean pajamas, adding a folded handkerchief in the pocket. Her most memorable activity was designed to protect my health. Every time she came to the apartment, she began by throwing open all the windows, then bustled through the rooms repeating her mantra, *"frische Luft, frische Luft"* (fresh air). In the bedrooms she threw the blankets and pillows over the windowsills to air while she did her other work. Her "frische Luft" certainly did freshen the apartment, bed, and bedclothes, but it also dropped the temperature temporarily almost to the temperature outside—cold indeed in February and March in Munich.

True to the warning I had received on accepting the apartment, in August 1955 I was required to move as my building was emptied and returned to its German owners. The Army had no more requisitioned apartments in Munich, but it still had many houses. I was offered a fully furnished and equipped three-bedroom residence at 62 Bruggsperger Strasse in Harlaching, not far from where the Aschenfelters had lived. Unfortunately, Frau Schiller came only once to clean this house. Quite upset, she said she was frightened because she saw a man go into our basement—a strange man who had a beard and looked like a Russian! He was, of course, the man hired by the Army to attend to the furnaces of all requisitioned houses in the vicinity. But nothing could change Frau Schiller's mind for she lived in fear of Russians. I had to find another cleaning woman from the Army's register.

My Cover Story

As I was moving into the house a pleasant incident occurred. I was unloading my car (the Mercedes diesel formerly assigned to Charlie O'Hearn) when the entire German family who lived next door—a married couple and their two teenage daughters—came out to bid me *willkommen* (welcome). With a warm smile, the older daughter handed me a bunch of flowers from their garden. The mother said that she and her daughters would be pleased to help me clean up the house. I accepted the daughters' help in unloading the car and thanked the whole family. They were very nice neighbors, but I saw little of them. Our schedules didn't match, and in any event, I wanted to avoid close contact lest they ask questions about me and my job—questions I did not want to answer.

But these questions could not be avoided completely. It was natural to wonder why a U.S. Navy officer was stationed in Munich, hundreds of miles from salt water. In general, Germans I met did not ask that question but I am sure they thought about it. When occasionally someone would ask, I would avoid answering by joking that I was the *Vizeadmiral der Isarflotte* (vice admiral of the Isar River Fleet.)

If questioning persisted I would say that I was a *Verbindungs Offizier* (liaison officer) between the Seventh Army headquarters and the U.S. Navy's port at Bremerhaven. If asked what I did, my most successful answer was to say that I did very little and had a wonderful time in Munich. Usually this was accepted as plausible, and the questioner, laughing, would tell of a friend who had had a good deal like mine in the German forces during World War II.

Max's Party

After a few weeks of work at Possart Platz 3, I had come to feel at ease working with the Germans of our office staff. I felt especially comfortable with Max Parnitzki, who, after about a month, invited me to a party at his apartment. He said that others from the office, his sister and her son who were visiting from Switzerland, and his mother would be at the party.

I was flattered by his invitation and wanted to accept it; it would certainly advance my relationship with our German staff. Still, I thought it best to postpone an answer until I could talk with the Skipper, for I did not know whether there was any policy at the office concerning fraternization with the German staff. The Skipper was, as usual, open-minded and helpful. When I told him about Max's invitation, his reply was a simple question, "Do you want to go?"

"Yes," I replied.

"Then go and enjoy yourself."

Max's apartment was at Klug Strasse 33 in the Nymphenburg area of Munich. It was the upper floor of a small, two-story house somewhat the worse for wear and far away from the gracious splendor of Possart Platz 3 and the grand houses and tree-lined streets of Bogenhausen. Max, his mother, his visiting sister, and her son were sharing the apartment. When I arrived the living room was already crowded with Max's family and his guests—Helmuth Pich, Fräulein Sellschopp, and Fräulein Kinshofer.

There was, of course, some stiffness and reserve at first. We stood around awkwardly addressing each other as "Leutnant Durning," "Herr Pich," or "Fräulein Sellschopp," too much on guard to make the party come alive. But that changed quickly; Max brought food, beer, and vodka from the kitchen, ingredients effective at melting away the reserve and loosening all tongues. Max welcomed everyone with "*Prosit*" (the traditional German toast) taken in vodka, not beer, and this was followed by food and "*Na zdarovye*," a traditional Russian toast of chilled vodka. Soon the room was abuzz with voices and laughter. My German improved immensely—or so it seemed to me—and I learned a great deal about my colleagues at work.

Max introduced me to his mother, a shy lady whose round and smiling face fit perfectly with her rather short and round figure. She spoke little and that little was in Russian. Max explained that his mother was Russian, and his father, who was deceased, was a German engineer who had been working in Kharkov in the northeast of Ukraine. There were two children of the marriage, Max and his sister.

After the vodka, Helmuth Pich and I found ourselves seated next to each other on a couch. He tried to light a cigarette, but through several attempts his lighter would not work, and he was forced to ask for a light from one of the other guests. Returning to the couch he said, "*Ab und zu funktioniert mein Feuer*" (From time to time my lighter works). I had never before heard the phrase "*ab und zu*," and so Helmuth's comment started an amusing conversation in which Helmuth attempted to teach me the phrase by using it in many different contexts. I tried some sentences myself and others joined in the game of teaching German to "Leutnant Durning." As we continued to consume the vodka, I soon became "Marveen" as they became "Max," "Helmuth," "Waldtraut," and "Toni." The barriers were down.

For me, much good flowed from Max's party: my German improved rapidly, thanks to my many teachers; in the office, our teamwork and productivity improved; I enjoyed some pleasant weekend excursions (*Ausflüge*) to beautiful and interesting places in Munich and Bavaria; I gained a much deeper understanding of Germany, central Europe, and the Soviet Union; and, most important, I formed lasting friendships. Indeed, I enjoyed my time in Bavaria so much that I jokingly called myself *ein adoptierter Bayer* (an adopted Bavarian) and sought to learn all I could of the region's history and culture.

Max shared my interest in history, and our conversations led us back to the entry of the earliest Germanic and Slavonic tribes into Europe from Scandinavia, the wanderings of the tribes, and their ever-growing pressure on the Roman Empire. Max was amazingly erudite about the Germanic tribes and generous in sharing his knowledge with me.

We spoke also of the deep, perhaps religious, bond between Germans and their land. Southern Germany is beautiful, a harmonious juncture of people and nature. The forests are abundant and green; the villages are well tended and clean. Germans often speak about *das Vaterland* (the Fatherland) as if it were a living thing. Once in the Black Forest, I saw a giant farmhouse for people and animals, built entirely of wood, sited atop a small rise, edged up against the dark green forest, with a lighter green meadow in front. Painted on the front gable over the doorway of the house in large letters was a short poetic prayer:

> Deutsches Haus, Deutsches Land
> Schirme Gott mit starker Hand
> (German house, German land
> God protect with a mighty hand)

Lengries

I remember with especial fondness an excursion we made to visit Toni Kinshofer at her family's home in Lengries, a typical Bavarian village with hardly a leaf out of place. The Kinshofers' house faced onto the village square. Toni gave us a tour, which ended in the big farm-style kitchen. I was especially impressed by the oven—a long rectangular box, about waist high and six feet wide, extending from one wall twelve to fifteen feet down to the middle of the kitchen. It was entirely covered by ceramic tiles, with openings to put in firewood and places for cooking pots on top. Where the oven reached the wall, a matching tile-covered stack ran up through the ceiling to warm the rooms above. Such great ovens were common in Bavaria. They were beautiful and radiated warmth. I can still picture us in the kitchen having coffee and *kuchen* (cake), joking about an imaginary war between Lengries and its neighbor Bad Tölz.

In the months following Max's party I learned more about my colleagues, especially Max Parnitzki and Helmuth Pich. Some of what I learned about their service in the German armed forces might easily have cooled our relationship, but instead our trust in each other grew.

9

MAX PARNITZKI

Max's life embodied the European experience of World War II, a war that killed perhaps 50 million people, turned great cities into rubble, uprooted and forcibly moved millions of people from their homes, disrupted plans, and denied hopes. Like millions of others, Max suffered keenly, but by his strength, intelligence, empathy for others, and fundamental morality, he overcame all and turned every adversity into an opportunity. Student, soldier, prisoner of war, multilinguist, helper of refugees, intelligence analyst, journalist, expert on Russian and Soviet bloc military and political affairs, husband, father, traveler, German loyalist, friend to his comrades—and judging no man to be his personal enemy—Max was all of these and more.

I met Max on my first day at Possart Platz 3 and worked collegially with him thereafter, translating and editing many hundreds of intelligence reports received from the Gehlen Organization and carrying out two interrogations of border crossers from the East bloc. This shared work began building the bridge between us, and the party at his home in the Klug Strasse removed most social barriers of age or nationality. From many long conversations during my time with the Navy in Munich and our later mutual visits, and from papers provided to me by Waldtraut, his wife, and Marion, his older daughter, I know the main elements of his challenging life.

Early Years

Max's father, Franz Parnitzki, was a German engineer who settled in Kharkov, a major city of Ukraine, before World War I but retained his German citizenship. He married a Russian woman. They had two children—Max, born March 13, 1919, and his sister Marion, seven years younger. After the Russian Revolution, Ukraine, including

Kharkov, became part of the Union of Soviet Socialist Republics (USSR), but because his father was German, Max maintained German citizenship.

Franz Parnitzki founded a factory to make construction machinery in Kharkov, but the Soviet Communist government expropriated it in the mid-1920s. After losing his factory, Franz worked as leading engineer for a large Ukrainian construction company. Economic and political conditions in the USSR went from bad to worse, and Franz developed serious health problems as well. In 1933 Franz Parnitzki and his family left Kharkov and moved to Berlin, where they hoped conditions would be better and better health care would be available. Franz Parnitzki's health worsened; he was hospitalized for a long time and died in 1943.

Max told me that after his family's move to Berlin, his father's bad health rendered him unable to work. This put the Parnitzkis in very difficult straits and forced Max's mother, who spoke little German, to work as a servant in homes of wealthy Berliners to support herself and her children.

Education and Entry into Military Service

Max grew up bilingual in German and Russian. His first schooling was with a private tutor, after which he completed eight years at the German middle school in Kharkov. Max was fourteen when the family moved to Germany in 1933; he studied four years at Berlin's German-Russian Realgymnasium and passed his *Abitur* examinations in 1937, when he was eighteen, to qualify for entry into a German university. With his Abitur done, Max did over seven months (March 3, 1937–October 20, 1937) *Reichsarbeitsdienst* (national labor service), and then he enlisted in the German Army. From the beginning of November 1937 to the beginning of World War II on September 1, 1939, Max served *Wehrdienst* (military defense service). This Wehrdienst included his basic training in the Army and assignment to an artillery regiment in Heilsberg, East Prussia. Wehrdienst changed to *Kriegsdienst* (war service) on September 1, 1939, when German troops invaded Poland and World War II began.

Max's school years in Berlin, 1933–37, and pre-war service years, 1937–39, were years of tumult, violence, and rapid change in Germany. Hitler became chancellor of Germany in January 1933, and the Nazi Party spread its control wider and tighter in the following years. In these years under Hitler, Germany openly violated its Versailles

Treaty obligations, rearmed on a giant scale, reoccupied the Rhineland, pressured Austria to annex to Germany, annexed the Czech Sudetenland to Germany and occupied the rest of Czechoslovakia, and demanded that Poland cede to Germany Danzig and a corridor from Germany across Poland to Danzig. In domestic affairs the Nazis escalated their persecution of Germany's Jews, Gypsies, Communists, and others, including violent attacks by the Nazi uniformed paramilitary Storm Troopers. The Nazis extended dictatorial control over the German people, their local governments, schools, universities, churches, and courts. The first concentration camps were opened.

Max could not have been unaware of these events, and I cannot help wondering what his thoughts were at that time. He never discussed this period of his life with me in detail, and his papers shed no light on his thoughts. Max told us that he had been a member of the Hitler Youth and had found the uniforms, music, and rallies exciting, as any teenaged young man would. Similarly, he once explained to me that in the Army the comradeship of his fellow soldiers and the exhilaration of synchronized marching and singing stirred his emotions. I understand such reactions to things military and patriotic; I believe that they are the same for young men and women in uniform throughout the world. They are natural—but dangerous—emotions.

To understand Max, we must recognize that from 1937 when he finished his Abitur until January 1950, twelve years in all, he lived as either a soldier or a prisoner of war. He fought on *die Ostfront* (the East Front, the battle line of the German invasion of Russia) in Poland and in the USSR. Max was twenty when the war began. His combat service—September 1939 to June 29, 1944, two months short of five years—was all on the East Front. Therefore, to know Max, we must know the main events of the war on the East Front.

German Invasion of Poland, September 1939

On September 1, 1939, the German Wehrmacht (armed forces), with no declaration of war, invaded Poland. The German *blitzkrieg* swept eastward and overwhelmed the Poles in one month's time. Not to be left out, on September 17, 1939, the Soviet Union invaded Poland and occupied the eastern half of the country.

German Invasion of the Soviet Union, Operation Barbarossa, June 22, 1941

The invasion of the Soviet Union on June 22, 1941—Operation

Barbarossa—set off a titanic struggle of almost four years' duration, involving millions of soldiers on both sides. Sir John Keegan, in his history *The Second World War*, describes the German forces that attacked the Soviet Union:

> On 14 June in "eastern and northern parts of Germany," . . . nearly four million German troops, organized in 180 divisions, with 3350 tanks and 7200 guns supported by 2000 aircraft, stood ready to march to war. They were to be accompanied by fourteen Romanian divisions and shortly to be joined by the Finnish, Hungarians and puppet Slovak armies, together with a volunteer Spanish (the "Blue") and several Italian divisions.

Stalin had numerous reports of the massive German buildup, but seeking to avoid any provocation and hoping to settle any German demands by diplomacy and concessions, his response was slow. When he finally ordered full mobilization, it was too late. Keegan's account continues:

> [On 22 June] the German offensive was upon them. Mass air raids and a gigantic artillery bombardment fell upon airfields and fortified zones. Behind this wall of fire the German Army in the east, the *Ostheer*, moved to the attack.[1]

The German attack was organized in three army groups: Army Group North, headed to take Leningrad; Army Group Center, driving to take Moscow; and Army Group South, headed to take Kiev and then turn southward to take the Crimea and the economic zone from Kiev to Stalingrad and to Kharkov.

Max was twenty-two when Operation Barbarossa was launched; he was a soldier in that giant invasion army, probably from its start. On July 13, 1941, only twenty days after the invasion, Max was awarded the Iron Cross Second Class (see appendix B). The certificate of this award was signed by the commander of Panzer Group 2. It appears that Max's radio intercept unit went into Russia with Panzer Group 2, which was part of the German Ninth Army and of Army Group Center headed for Moscow.

---

1. John Keegan, *The Second World War* (New York: Penguin Books, 1989), 181.

Max seldom discussed his war assignments but summarized them later in his curriculum vitae (see appendix A). His basic training and part of his service was with the Artillery Regiment (2./A.R. 11) based originally in Heilsberg, East Prussia. He was soon transferred to monitoring enemy radio communications, i.e., intercepting Russian Army radio transmissions, decoding and translating them into German for the German commanders. He served in a number of different units and locations, including a fixed listening station in Königsberg, and a number of mobile monitoring units moving with the advancing German lines. Max described to me mobile army units that could race out ahead of the German lines to find and tap Russian Army telephone lines, listen to the Russian communications, translate them to German, and relay the information back to the oncoming German commanders.

The Tide Turns

The war on the East Front went well for the Germans in 1941, but they were stopped short of both Leningrad and Moscow by fierce resistance and the arrival of the Russian winter. They resumed the offensive in the spring of 1942, and Hitler diverted some forces from Army Group Center and directed a battle to take the Russian city, Stalingrad. Both sides sustained fierce fighting and endured heavy losses. The Soviet army put up violent resistance and broke out to surround the attacking Germans. With this battle the tide on the East Front turned and the Soviet army went over to the offensive.

In July 1943 the advancing Soviet forces defeated the German army in the titanic battle of Kursk.

> The armour continued to mass and move on a scale unlike anything seen anywhere else in the war . . . tank armadas on the move. . . . Almost 4000 Soviet tanks and nearly 3000 German tanks and assault guns . . . drawn into this gigantic battle.[2]

Soviet forces went on in 1943 and 1944 to recover all of their lost territories. In their advance, the Soviets smashed the German Ninth Army in the southern sector of Army Group Center's front. Max's unit was surrounded.

---

2. John Erickson, quoted in Keegan, *The Second World War*, 468.

Max Is Captured

On June 29, 1944, Max was wounded and captured. In his curriculum vitae Max wrote,

> My military career led me after the completion of basic and field training with an artillery unit in East Prussia, to the signal corps and to various radio monitoring units (radio interception intelligence). In late June 1944, when the beaten 9th German Army was trying to break out of the Soviet encirclement in Byelorussia, I was wounded and taken prisoner of war by the Soviet Army. With a group of 700 or 800 wounded German POWs I was marched to a Soviet field hospital at NOVOYYBKOV.

Max was twenty-five years old when he became a prisoner of war. He had been a soldier for seven years (1937–44). He had been promoted three times, ending as a *Wachtmeister* (sergeant).

POW: Five and a Half Years in the USSR, June 29, 1944–January 2, 1950

Millions of soldiers, German and Russian, were killed, wounded, or taken prisoner on the East Front. A large portion of the wounded and the imprisoned died but their fate remains unknown; they are listed in the records as "missing in action." Max never spoke to me at length about his feelings at the time of his capture. He did say that when he was lying wounded in tall grass, he thought he might be dying and could think only of his mother. Fortunately he received medical care from the Russian Army.

Max spoke often of his life as a POW, and the document included herein as Appendix A was given to me by his family during my visit to Munich in May–June 2004. The undated document, titled "Brief Curriculum Vitae and Experience as a Prisoner of War in the USSR," was written by Max in English after his return to Germany. The subject matter, the style, and the fact that it is in English and typewritten lead me to think that he meant it for delivery to an American agency, perhaps as part of his security screening in connection with his work for the U.S. Navy at Possart Platz 3. The document is filled with information about Max's life and duties as a POW. It also demonstrates his excellent command of English. Max's document is short but reveals a great deal about him, including his intelligence and his unwavering courage under pressure and threats from Communist political officers seeking his cooperation. It shows also his skills at languages and the open, friendly relation he was able to establish with some of the Russian officers running some of the camps for German POWs.

Max as Authorized Horse Thief

Max told some stories concerning the lighter side of his POW life: how he became a successful horse thief and how he learned English.

In the last year of the war and the first few postwar years, food was very scarce both for the Russian civilian population and for the prisoners of war. Meat especially was in very short supply. One day in the early evening, the POW camp saw a great herd of horses coming across the nearby fields, driven by a small detail of Russian soldiers. The whole herd stopped for the night in an area of deep grass and a stream not far from the prison camp. Early the next morning the herd moved on, only to be followed a few days later by another such herd.

The commander of the POW camp called Max to his office and to Max's surprise asked, "Can you ride a horse?"

Max replied quickly, "Yes."

"Good! Report here at nine this evening. We're going to get a horse and ride it back to camp. Tell no one about this."

Darkness fell. Max reported promptly at 9:00 p.m. The commander, holding a rope, and Max set out across the fields to the deep grass where the horses had spread out while grazing. They singled out a horse alone at the edge of the herd, quietly slipped a rope halter over its head, and led it away a short distance out of sight of the soldiers. They both mounted the horse and rode it back to the camp. Outside the camp kitchen, with the help of the camp cooks, they killed the horse, butchered it, sent the meat to the kitchen to be cooked at once, and buried the bones, offal, and all inedible parts of the horse. The next day the whole camp had meat.

The passing of great herds of horses continued every few days for a month or so, and each time the commander and Max brought back meat. Unfortunately for the POWs' nutrition, the herds stopped passing.

Learning English

Max's method of learning English was unusual. Early in his captivity, the wife of his POW camp commander loaned Max her Russian-English dictionary. Max copied the whole dictionary, word-by-word on any paper he could find. The wherewithal for his practice at reading

English came from American lend-lease aid to the Soviet Union during the war. Max and other POWs were put to work unpacking boxes in which American equipment had been sent to Russia. The packing around the equipment was usually old American newspapers. The prisoners treasured these crumpled and outdated newspapers, for they were the only source of news of the outside world other than Soviet propaganda. To Max they became his English textbook. With constant practice and help from a fellow prisoner who spoke English, Max turned his adversity to good purpose, replacing some of the university education the war had stolen from him. Ever seeing the humor in life, at Possart Platz 3 Max sometimes asked me to forgive a mistake in one of his translations of an intelligence report, saying he spoke and wrote like an American newspaper.

Release from Prison Camp, January 2, 1950

In his "Brief Curriculum Vitae and Experience as a Prisoner of War in the USSR" Max describes his transfers from camp to camp from June to December 1949 as camps were being closed and the POWs were sent back to Germany. He writes,

> Finally, all remaining POWs who were not sentenced to hard labor for alleged war crimes were concentrated again in the camp No. 7168/11 and thence dismissed to Germany in October, November, and December 1949. I was released with the second to last group on January 2, 1950.

Max may have been in error in thinking that all German POWs except war criminals were released in 1949, or he may have been speaking of only those collected in the camp where he was. I asked Max why he had been held so long, and he replied, "They were extra suspicious of me because I spoke Russian. Perhaps I was a spy or a Russian citizen who had defected to the Germans. The same kind of worries about me had been entertained at first by the German Army, but their worries disappeared as my officers got to know me."

International Refugee Organization, 1950–52

Returned to Germany in the first days of January 1950, Max found a job with the International Refugee Organization in Munich and worked there until 1952. He started as a driver in the Transport Division and rose through several promotions to be the transport officer supervising all drivers, taxi dispatching, and vehicle utilization. In January 1952 his supervisor, the zone operations officer, wrote a letter in praise of Max:

> Capable of accepting more and more responsibility . . . carried out every task efficiently and conscientiously . . . complete satisfaction . . . can thoroughly recommend . . . have no doubt that he will acquit himself to the entire satisfaction . . .

Val Rychly met Max through his work at the refugee camps and recognized his talents and potential. He hired Max in January 1952 for work at Possart Platz 3.

10

HELMUTH PICH

Nothing in our backgrounds could predict that Helmuth Pich and I would become friends. He was at least a decade older than I was, a Prussian, and in the true Junker tradition, sought a career in military service. Nevertheless, we worked well together at Possart Platz 3 and shared some hours together outside of work.

Helmuth was a bachelor when we worked together. His pay was modest and he lived quite modestly—undoubtedly quite a comedown from his wartime situation as a pilot and submarine commander. He lived in a rented room in the apartment of a Bavarian couple. He kept bread, cheese, and sausages in his room and made breakfasts and sometimes sandwiches for lunch. From time to time, he led Max and me to an affordable restaurant he had found. One of his favorites was a restaurant in the Sendlinger Strasse featuring large plates of North Sea fish with potato salad (*Seelachs mit Kartoffelsalat*). It was a crowded, noisy place with large tables and benches where customers were crowded together in a friendly way and no formality existed. Plates were piled high with fish and potato salad and washed down with cold Munich beer. We liked the place, the food, and the reasonable price. The presence of the large Nordsee Company refrigerator trucks that brought in fresh fish from the North Sea was additional evidence of German economic recovery, another part of the Wirtschaftswunder.

Helmuth entered the German Navy as a teenager and worked up through the various Navy schools to become an officer and then a naval aviator. During the first years of the war, after the German army took most of the Balkans, Helmuth's naval air unit was based in Greece. He told of this duty with enthusiasm, describing the pleasure of flying reconnaissance flights over the Mediterranean under bright sun and brilliant blue skies. There was, he said with a smile, "little fighting and many beautiful days . . . almost a holiday from the war."

But all that changed in 1942 as Germany stepped up its U-boat campaign against Allied shipping in the Atlantic and Caribbean. Officers and crews were urgently needed to man the increasing number of U-boats and to replace the crews lost in the intense battle of the Atlantic sea-lanes. Helmuth volunteered and entered into the elite German U-boat service, rising to command a submarine.

His experiences in World War II were the subject of many conversations during which we grew more and more comfortable with each other. All soldiers and sailors have war stories to tell; Helmuth Pich's tales are dramatic. He had flown over Greece, taken a submarine from the Battle of the Atlantic to Indonesia, and been captured by the Royal Dutch Navy.

Helmuth's U-Boat in the Battle of the Atlantic

The Battle of the Atlantic was a life or death struggle for Britain as the German Navy and Luftwaffe sought to sink the merchant ships bringing supplies to the United Kingdom and thus strangle the British war effort. From the beginning of the war in 1939 until December 1941, the commander of the German U-boat fleet concentrated his attacks in the eastern Atlantic, respecting the U.S. coastal waters as neutral.

After the Japanese attack on Pearl Harbor and Hitler's declaration of war against the United States, Germany treated the United States as an enemy combatant and sent submarines off the Atlantic Coast of North America and into the Gulf of Mexico. For a few months these U-boats had great success, sinking hundreds of thousands of tons of coastwise shipping, including tankers bringing Texas and Louisiana oil to the U.S. East Coast and merchant ships of all kinds coming down the Mississippi River from the port of New Orleans to its mouth, out into the Gulf of Mexico and thence to Britain, Russia, and ports all over the world.

Several months after Max's party Helmuth told me he commanded a submarine that had patrolled off Cuba and off the mouth of the Mississippi River and had sunk a number of ships. He showed me photos taken from the conning tower of his U-boat, one of which showed a burning tanker off the mouth of the river. This was particularly meaningful to me because I grew up in New Orleans and my mother was a Red Cross volunteer called out night or day to assist in caring for survivors of such sunken ships. The photo was worth more than a thousand words to both of us. It was a test of our relationship.

We talked about it and agreed that we would not let it spoil our friendship.

Helmuth's U-boat as Freighter to Japan

Helmuth had an unusual assignment during the war: to take his submarine halfway around the world to Japanese-occupied Indonesia and then serve as a freighter carrying scarce war supplies to Japan. Helmuth received this assignment late in the war, when both Germany and Japan were feeling the effects of the combined Allied naval power. American submarines and aircraft had succeeded in blockading Japan so effectively that scarcely any Japanese merchant ships could bring supplies to the Japanese home islands. Hitler had promised help to Japan and sent submarines to serve as freighters. Helmuth's boat was ordered to the Pacific to help.

As Helmuth told it, for most of the way the voyage was like a South Seas cruise. Leaving European waters, he avoided all the usual Atlantic trade routes and traveled through the vast South Atlantic, an ocean so empty that he occasionally allowed the crew to sunbathe and swim in the warm, tropical waters. Helmuth navigated his U-boat to a planned rendezvous with a German tanker and supply ship somewhere in the South Atlantic. Refueled and resupplied, he maneuvered eastward around Africa's southernmost tip, the Cape of Good Hope, and entered the Indian Ocean. Again avoiding the shipping lanes, he continued for days without encountering any ship or plane, until one day his luck ran out.

Helmuth explained, "We had surfaced to recharge our batteries and were making good progress on the surface when we heard a faint buzzing sound from the sky ahead—a sound like a mosquito flying nearby in the quiet of the night. Everyone became alert at once and searched the skies. The buzz grew louder. To the east we saw the source of the buzz—an airplane!—coming directly at us! Emergency alarms were sounded in the sub and I gave the order to *tauchen* [dive] at once."

Helmuth and his crew had not needed to discuss the nature or intentions of the plane for no planes friendly to Germany flew over the Indian Ocean. There were only British or American planes from aircraft carriers or island bases. "The race was on! My crew ran to battle stations; all hatches were closed; the sub was trimmed for its steepest possible emergency dive, and it quickly started down. The plane came on at top speed, too, and the result was almost a draw. My

U-boat went fully under and steeply down, but the plane arrived on target in time to see our course and drop a pattern of depth charges. Then the plane circled and attacked us again. We survived the first attack, but with some damage; we dived deep, turned, and escaped without damage from the second attack."

That was not the end. Hours later, after night had fallen, the sub surfaced again many miles from where it had encountered the plane. The U-boat recharged batteries, took in fresh air, and completed its damage assessment. The damage was serious but not disabling, and the submarine continued its voyage by night, steering for Jakarta, Indonesia, where the Japanese, who had taken Indonesia from the Dutch early in the war, had ship repair facilities.

Helmuth's sub made it to Jakarta and went into the yard for repairs. The repairs took several weeks, and a new threat arose. The patrol plane had obviously reported its encounter; a full-scale search had ensued and the British discovered the submarine in the Jakarta shipyard. A small flotilla of Royal Navy and Free Dutch destroyers and submarines were blockading the harbor's entrance, waiting for Helmuth's submarine to come out. Allied agents ashore watched for any signs that the sub would move.

The End of the Trip

"Repairs completed, we took on a cargo of rubber to be carried to Japan," Helmuth said. "I had no choice; we had to leave the harbor, escape the waiting warships, and go on to Japan."

He tried. At the darkest time of the night, in complete silence, they cast off their mooring lines and headed out to sea. But fortune did not smile on them. They were discovered, fired on, and then rammed by a Dutch submarine. Helmuth's sub started to sink but the crew had just enough time to escape. They were rescued and taken aboard the Dutch submarine as prisoners of war.

At first, as Helmuth told his story, they were treated strictly as enemy prisoners, but after a day or two the Dutch and German submariners began to talk, finding common interest in comparing their submarines and naval life. They recognized the invisible bonds that tie together all submariners, everywhere.

They were taken to a prisoner-of-war camp in Australia, where they stayed until the end of the war. Of this experience, Helmuth said, "I liked Australia. The Australians treated us well, and sent us home to Germany promptly when the fighting ended."

Helmuth was indeed lucky, for in World War II two out of three German submariners lost their lives, and casualties, including wounded, were 75 percent overall.[1]

---

1. John Keegan, *The Second World War* (New York: Penguin Books, 1989), 107.

11

ERIKA MÜLLER

In the months following Max's party, Max, Helmuth, and I made several Saturday or Sunday excursions to nearby lakes and mountains. Sometimes Waldtraut Sellschopp accompanied us, but Toni Kinshofer went each weekend to see her family in Lengries.

On several occasions Helmuth brought along a friend, Erika Müller (not her real name), a young woman who was a refugee from the Soviet occupied zone. Erika was a lovely young woman in her twenties. She worked as a drafter in an architect's office and lived in a rented room in the apartment of a Bavarian family. Taller and slimmer than average Bavarian girls, with the finely chiseled and symmetrical features we see in fashion models, Erika matched her elegant looks with a warm and vivacious personality. Erika's looks had not protected her in life, however.

Erika and Helmuth were opposites in personality—he, quiet and reserved, she outgoing and effusive. They were friends but did not seem to be romantically involved. Erika had a quick wit and was a keen observer. She told us that the flower patterns embroidered across the bodice of the Bavarian girls' dirndls matched the flowers in boxes on the fronts of the Bavarian houses; both were *Blumen auf den Balkon* (flowers on the balcony). On seeing a noisy group of stocky young men in lederhosen strutting alongside a street in one of the Bavarian towns, she burst out with a delighted laugh, exclaiming, "*Schau' mal: die Dorf-Bullen!*" (Look: the village bulls!)

I liked Erika, and she appeared to like me. Gradually, over a period of a few months, she told us more and more about herself. In 1945 as the East Front collapsed and the Soviet Army came ever nearer, even teenage German boys and girls were called up for war service, the boys as frontline soldiers, the girls in other roles. Erika was assigned to duty on an antiaircraft gun and sat many nights in the freezing cold awaiting the arrival of the Allied bombers that were systematically destroying German rail yards, factories, and cities. And then came the Soviet Army. In the words of Professor John Erickson, "Speed, frenzy and savagery characterized the advance. Villages and small towns burned, while Soviet soldiers raped at will and wreaked an atavistic vengeance."[1]

Once, over coffee, Erika told us the story of her escape to West Germany. As the Soviet Army arrived, she and her sister ran to hide in their house, but they were seen by a Russian soldier who ran after them and began to break down their front door. Just in time a Russian officer arrived, saw what was happening and ordered the soldier away from the house. Speaking in halting, imperfect German, he told Erika's mother that he understood her fear for her daughters, for he had daughters himself. He advised her that they should stay out of sight and hide as best they could; he had to move on and could not stay to protect them.

Erika, her sister, and her mother gathered what food and warm clothes they had and, when night fell, left on foot to walk to safety in the West. Hiding by day and at every approach of Soviet troops, they walked for several nights. Finally they escaped to territory occupied by the Allied armies. Wiping her eyes, Erika looked at me and said through her tears, "Entschuldigen, Marvin, ich sollte nicht weinen. Das ist alles vorbei und ich bin hier." (Excuse me, Marvin, I should not cry. That is all over now and I am here.)

The Telephone Tap

In May or June 1955 the Skipper asked me to come to his office, and after I entered, he closed the door and picked up a piece of paper from his desk. "Who is Erika Müller?" he asked.

"A friend of Helmuth Pich. She has been with us several times in our excursions in Munich or to the mountains."

"Friend or girlfriend?"

"Friend only, I think, but I really don't know."

"Read this," he said and handed me the piece of paper he had been holding. "Why is she asking about you?"

The paper was a transcription of a telephone conversation between

---

1. Quoted in John Keegan, *The Second World War* (New York: Penguin Books, 1989), 512.

Helmuth and Erika. Helmuth was phoning from his office to invite Erika to some event or excursion, and she asked several times, "Kommt Herr Durning mit?" (Is Mr. Durning coming?)

"Now listen to this," he said, switching on a tape recorder. Their voices were clear. They said precisely the words in the transcript. Erika was very persistent in her queries about me. "Why is she asking about you?"

"I don't know, but it appears that she wants to see me. I guess an American bachelor officer having a Mercedes sedan can be a person of interest to a young and unmarried German woman who fled her home as a refugee from the Russians."

"You are probably right, but still we must be careful. Helmuth is OK, but we'll have to check on Fräulein Müller. Don't say anything to anyone about this. Just carry on naturally, just as you would have done before I showed you this."

I was shocked. There was a tap on Helmuth's office phone line and probably on other lines, too—maybe on all the lines in the office. Perhaps the offices were bugged. Maybe O'Hearn and Aschenfelter were right after all. But maybe not. "Wait, listen, don't jump to conclusions," I thought.

I'm glad I waited, for the matter was resolved in a week or so, when the Skipper again called me to his office and said, "Everything is all right. Erika Müller has a clean record." Smiling now, he added, "Her interest in you seems to be from passion, not politics. Be careful—passion can be dangerous too."

I never asked the Skipper about the phone tap or possible bugs, and he never volunteered any explanation. I had no need to know. My guess, however, is that he had arranged a general tap on the office phones with the U.S. Army Counter Intelligence Corps (CIC), for later the Skipper called on the CIC to sweep our offices for bugs and told me he did so from time to time.

Erika's Letter

Several weeks later, I invited our little group—Max, Waldtraut, Helmuth, and Erika—to my apartment in the Schumann Strasse for drinks before we went to dinner at the Hofbräuhaus Festhalle. Erika seemed nervous, distracted, or even sad about something. She followed me to the kitchen when I went to pour the drinks and, standing quite near to me, took one of my hands in hers and said, "Listen to me. I want to talk with you." But just then Max came into the kitchen to remind us that it was almost time to leave.

Possart Platz 3, the office of U.S. Naval Intelligence in Munich.
Marvin Durning, May 2004

Apartment building on Schumann Strasse in Bogenhausen.
Jean Durning, May 2004

Johannes R. Becher, Minister of Culture of the Deutsche Demokratische Republik (DDR) speaking in Munich. Münchner Illustrierte, 30 July 1955, photo by Heinz Hering

Deutsche Tragödie:

Wir verstehen uns nicht mehr

„Ich hoffe, daß ich Sie nicht enttäuschen werde." Mit diesem Satz begann Johannes R. Becher, Schriftsteller und Kulturminister der DDR (Bild unten), die erste Diskussion, die in Westdeutschland mit einem Mitglied des Sowjetzonen-Kabinetts geführt wurde. Der Münchner Buchhändler Ernst Ludwig hatte den Minister zu seinen „Scholastika-Gesprächen" eingeladen. Becher, gebürtiger Münchner, pries in geschicktem Formulierungen die Vorzüge des östlichen Regierungssystems und rief in den überfüllten Saal: „Wir müssen wieder lernen, miteinander zu reden, wenn sich die beiden Deutschland nicht völlig auseinanderleben sollen." Gleich darauf erklärte er, es sei unrentabel, sich um das historisch notwendigen Kommunismus herumzudrücken. Kulturelle Zusammenarbeit sei die Grundlage für eine Wiedervereinigung. Als der freie Verkauf westlicher Zeitungen und Bücher als erster Schritt gefordert wurde, lehnte Becher ab. „Dann geben Sie zu, daß im Osten keine Freiheit herrscht!" forderte ein Zwischenrufer. Nach drei Stunden endete das Gespräch ergebnislos. Man redete aneinander vorbei. Keiner hatte dem anderen einen annehmbaren Vorschlag machen können.

Erich Kuby, Publizist, warf Becher vor, daß er nur Tendenzliteratur zulasse. „Kul-

Joseph Scholmer, Autor, bezichtigte Becher der Schönfärberei. Was der Osten

Ernst J. Salter, Publizist, forderte die Wiederherstellung der Freiheit in der

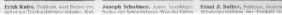

West German critics of lack of freedom in East Germany. Münchner Illustrierte, 30 July 1955, photo by Heinz Hering

General Reinhard Gehlen and his intelligence staff, the Wehrmacht Counterintelligence Unit, on the East Front in World War II. Photo © Bettmann/CORBIS

Lieutenant Commander Vladimir Rychly aboard U.S. aircraft carrier of the Sixth Fleet in the Mediterranean with General Adolf Heusinger and other officers. Photo courtesy of Hannelore Rychly

Waldtraut and Max Parnitzki with family in Hamburg on their wedding day. Photo courtesy of Waldtraut Parnitzki

Max Parnitzki. Photo courtesy of Waldtraut Parnitzki

Marvin Durning, Max Parnitzki, and Jean Durning at Parnitzki home in Meckenheim-Merl near Bonn. Waldtraut Parnitzki, October 1978

Marvin Durning with Helmuth and Hildegard Pich in the garden of their home in Geesthacht, near Hamburg. Jean Durning, May 1996

James Critchfield at Val Rychly's home in Neu Grünwald. Photo courtesy of Hannelore Rychly

James Critchfield, Hannelore Rychly, Val Rychly, and Frau Erna Mattheus at Rychly home in Neu Grünwald. Photo courtesy of Lois Critchfield, December 1977

Frau Mattheus, Hannelore Rychly, and Val Rychly at home in Neu Grünwald. Jean Durning, fall 1985

Marvin Durning, Jean Durning, Val Rychly, and Frau Mattheus in garden of the Rychly house in Neu Grünwald. Hannelore Rychly, May 1988

Lois and James Critchfield and Hannelore Rychly at reunion with children of
General Reinhard Gehlen at Hannelore Rychly's home in Neu Grünwald.
Photo courtesy of Hannelore Rychly, May 1998

The Hofbräuhaus Festhalle is no place for quiet conversation. It is a large room filled with large tables, the walls decorated by flags, and a Bavarian "oom-pah-pah" band playing at one end of the hall. Bavarians knew all the songs—in Bayerisch—and the rest of us learned a few. When the band struck up a favorite, everyone in the room rose, linked arms with their neighbors at the table, and swayed from side to side together (*schunkle*-ing) while singing the words. To end each set of songs, the band struck up the best-known and most popular song of all, "*In München steht ein Hofbräuhaus*" (In Munich stands a Hofbräuhaus). With a beer or two it was great fun.

During the whole evening Erika tried to be her usual cheerful self, but from time to time her spirits drooped and she looked as if she were going to cry. I wondered what was troubling her, but we never had a chance to talk.

Early the next morning, as I was leaving for work, I found a letter lying on the hallway floor in front of my door. I picked it up, opened it, and found it was from Erika. I went back into the apartment, closed the door, and sat down to read it. Everything about the letter said "Erika"—light blue paper, a flowing feminine handwriting, and a style both courteous and intense. However, I was shocked by the message.

Erika wrote that she could not sleep so she rose early to put into a letter what she had wanted to tell me personally the previous evening. She said that since she met me she had wanted to know me better. Several months had passed, and her feelings had grown so strong that she had to tell me that she loved me and wanted to be with me. She gave me her office and home telephone numbers and asked that I call her as soon as possible after reading her letter because she could think of nothing else. She prayed that we might meet that same evening after work and let her have the conversation she wanted, indeed needed, to explain herself.

I was shocked and deeply moved by her sincere and courageous letter. I recognized that Erika must have ridden trolleys and buses across Munich in the very early hours of the morning to put the letter at my door before she had to ride miles again to her workplace. I read the letter several times and did not know what I should do. I must confess that I even wondered whether this was part of a trap set for me as a means of penetrating our office. I hated myself for thinking about Erika in such a way, but I could not help it. I put the letter in my pocket and went to work.

When the Skipper arrived, I went to his office, closed the door behind me, and told him I needed some advice about the latest turn of events concerning Erika Müller. I told him the background and gave him the letter to read. We discussed what I should do. "Are you in love with her?" he asked.

"No, but I like her."

"Do you want to have an affair with her?"

"I don't know, but I don't want to cause trouble with Helmuth."

To my surprise the Skipper wasn't upset. He took the matter of my relationship with Erika seriously, especially because it could come to involve Helmuth and our working relationship. He did not think Erika was setting a trap; he saw an easier explanation. The situation of young German women was very difficult, and bachelor American officers often looked to them like knights in shining armor come to save them. Sexual mores in postwar Germany were much more liberal than in the United States then, and some German women had become bold in initiating relationships with men. In earlier years other Americans in the Munich office had become involved with German women. A young woman "Ushi" (Ursula) still came sometimes to the office, although her former partner, an American Marine assigned to the office, was long gone back to the States.

The Skipper's advice was that I do what I felt was right but not let Erika move in with me and beware of offending Helmuth.

I called Erika at her workplace and arranged to meet her for dinner that night. After dinner we went to my apartment to talk. It was an emotional evening for both of us. Erika cried sometimes and laughed at other times. She told me of the drabness of her life. She had a low paying and boring job with uninteresting people; she lived in one small rented room; she was from an educated middle-class family whose survivors had lost everything when they fled the Soviet Army and saw no prospect of getting anything back. She was many years younger than Helmuth, liked him but saw him only occasionally and only as a friend. She loved me, knew I was not in love with her, but hoped I would come to love her if we lived together for a while. With a mischievous smile, Erika added her final argument. She said she wanted me to take her to bed.

I liked Erika very much. I felt terrible when she cried and held her close, wishing I had a magic wand to take away all her troubles and pain. I respected her honesty and her courage. I sympathized with the difficulty of her situation but had to tell her I was not a knight in shining armor and could not offer myself as a cure for her problems. Regardless,

Erika stayed the night, and I drove her home in the morning.

A few weeks later, Helmuth told me that Erika had left Munich to join her sister and look for a better job in one of the north German cities.

12

FREEDOM TO PUBLISH: EAST AND WEST

It happened a half century ago, but I remember one summer evening in July 1955 as if it were yesterday.

Felix Heidenberger was a young journalist and freelance writer in Munich. I was introduced to him by a letter from his brother, who had emigrated from Germany to the United States and lived in Washington, D.C. I contacted Felix shortly after my arrival in Munich and struck up a friendly connection, nourished by Christmas letters and my occasional visits to Munich, that has lasted many years.

Felix was very bright and of cheerful disposition. He lived an active life—skiing in winter, sailing in summer, and spending nights out with his friends all year round. I enjoyed a number of evenings with Felix out and about Munich.

Felix introduced me to Harald Kubens, one of his journalist friends, during one of Harald's visits to Munich. Harald was a warm and outgoing person, a journalist working for the German news agency Deutsche Presse Agentur in its Paris office. Conversations with Felix and Harald were for me lessons in the politics of Germany and, indeed, of Europe.

There were, of course, two Germanys, the Federal Republic of Germany (Bundesrepublik Deutschland or West Germany) with its capital in Bonn and the German Democratic Republic (Deutsche Demokratische Republik or East Germany) with its capital in East Berlin. The gap between them widened each year with the growing intensity of the Cold War.

In July 1955 Johannes R. Becher, writer and minister of culture of the German Democratic Republic, was scheduled to speak in Munich. It was a big event, the first time a cabinet minister of the East German government would speak in West Germany. The event was sponsored by Ernst Ludwig, head of a prominent Munich book company, who, in the interest of a free and democratic Germany, sponsored a series of discussions named *Scholastika Gespräche* (Scholastika conversations) on important matters that might otherwise not be considered in public.

Minister Becher gave his speech in a hall in the old section of Munich, accessible on foot through dark, narrow, cobblestone streets. Felix Heidenberger, Harald Kubens, and I arrived at the meeting hall that July day to find a crowd at the entrance and a burly guard at the door, shouting that the hall was full. Undaunted, Felix pushed past the waiting crowd, motioning to Harald and to me to follow. Felix and Harald were journalists; they showed their press cards to the guard, who made no objection to their entrance. But I had no press card. To my amazement and amusement, Felix told the guard that I was an important American visitor, the son of the governor of Alabama! And so the guard let me in, too.

The hall was indeed full. Every seat was taken, people were standing in the aisles, and others sat on the sills of the deeply recessed windows. At the front of the hall stood a speaker's table with many microphones, and behind the table was an elevated stage. Felix quickly spotted the stage and led us to it. We climbed up and sat on the edge of the stage facing the audience, our feet dangling over the edge, not far from the backs of whoever might sit at or stand behind the speaker's table.

There was a noisy tension in the room. At last Minister Becher arrived, surrounded by a group of aides and bodyguards, all led by the sponsor of the meeting, Herr Ludwig. Minister Becher and Herr Ludwig took their places at the table. Herr Ludwig introduced Minister Becher and thanked him for coming to Munich. The audience grew quiet as Minister Becher rose to speak.

Minister Becher began slowly and carefully, stating how important it was that the two Germanys be able to speak to and understand one another. He turned then, however, to familiar themes of the Communist propaganda line, saying that East Germany was building a new and better Germany in cooperation with the Soviet Union and the other "socialist states"; that literature and all the arts flourished in the new socialist society; that East Germany was home to many highly talented young writers who would create the new and healthy socialist German literature of the future, in contrast to the decadent and fascist literature of West Germany and its capitalist allies, which were publishing the memoirs of former Nazi generals and making accusations of warmongering against the peace-loving socialist bloc.

Murmurs of disapproval or protest grew in the audience as the minister spoke. By the time Becher stopped the room was full of angry tension. Herr Ludwig asked for questions and comments from the audience, and many people lined up at the several microphones provided. Much was said in defense of free speech in the West and in criticism of the suppression of novels and other writing in the East. One speaker asked when the sale of West German books and newspapers would be permitted in East Germany; another read off the names of a number of East German writers whose books had been denied publication in the East because they did not follow the Communist Party line in all respects. Minister Becher became more and more visibly angry at the questions. Some questions he did not answer; he merely repeated his attack on what he called the Nazi or fascist nature of West German publications.

A man walked slowly to a microphone. He spoke slowly and quietly. He was a writer, he said, and had only recently returned to West Germany. He thanked Minister Becher for his remarks, which had stated clearly the policies of the East German state toward literature and the arts. He especially wanted to praise the minister's statement that there were many talented young East German writers; that statement was true, and he knew a number of these writers personally; he had seen them and talked with them many times over a long period until only recently. Then, taking a deep breath, and pausing between each name, he spoke slowly and clearly the names of five or six young writers, whose works were suppressed in East Germany and said, "I saw them and spoke with them daily until only a few weeks ago, for we were together—in Gulag Vorkuta."

At the end of this speech, a rumble of barely controlled anger rose from the audience. The Germans had all heard of the infamous Soviet concentration camp above the Arctic Circle at Vorkuta. Minister Becher rose, his face flushed, his voice tense, and said that socialist East Germany would never permit the publication of writings opposing the socialist state. His voice rising almost to a shout, he cried out, "Wir dürfen nicht erlauben das man schreibt was er will!" (We cannot allow someone to write whatever he wants!)

The next day the front page of the *Suddeutsche Zeitung*, published in Munich and one of the largest newspapers in Germany, carried a headline over its report of Becher's speech: "WIR DÜRFEN NICHT ERLAUBEN DAS MAN SCHREIBT WAS ER WILL."

My attendance at Minister Becher's talk had a surprising and amusing consequence. Shortly after the event, in the July 30, 1955 issue of a popular Munich publication, the *Münchner Illustrierte*, was a full-page report of the minister's visit with photos. The largest photo was of Minister Becher, taken from in front of the speaker's table; it included the faces of Marvin Durning, Harald Kubens, and one of the minister's bodyguards. The camera had missed Felix.

13

SOME VIGNETTES ABOUT GERMANY

The German Tribes

The first Germanic tribes entered central Europe more than two thousand years ago. They came from north of the Baltic—from present-day Scandinavia—and they came in waves for about a thousand years, ending with the Viking invasions of about 800 AD. The tribes moved about and fought over land across Europe. They took and held most of the land north of the Alps, between the Rhine and the Vistula, in the area we now call Germany.

Not until the late nineteenth century did Prussia, in a series of short wars under the leadership of Bismarck, unite most of the Germans in one political nation. In his introduction to Reinhard Gehlen's book *The Service*, George Bailey writes that Bismarck, when proclaiming the new German Empire began his address: "The German people, united in its tribes . . . "[1]

Perhaps the strongest division among the tribes was between the Prussians and the Bavarians. As explained by Barbara Tuchman in *The Proud Tower*,

> Berlin meant Prussia, the natural enemy of Munich and Bavaria. The North German regarded the South German as easy-going and self-indulgent, a sentimentalist who tended to be deplorably democratic, even liberal. In his turn, the South German regarded the North German as an arrogant bully with bad manners and an insolent stare who was

---

1. George Bailey, introduction to *The Service: The Memoirs of General Reinhard Gehlen*, by Reinhard Gehlen, trans. David Irving (New York: Word Publishing, 1972), xvii.
2. Barbara Tuchman, *The Proud Tower: A Portrait of the World Before the War, 1890–1914* (New York: Ballantine Books, 1962), 302.

politically reactionary and aggressively preoccupied with business.[2]

Even in 1955 the German people were still, culturally at least, tribal in their loyalties, reflecting their history of living in separate duchies, free cities, and some larger kingdoms such as Austria, Prussia, and Bavaria. They spoke different German dialects, sometimes dressed differently, and had different cultural and religious traditions.

Sind Sie Preusse?

I had one experience that showed that some Bavarians still cherished a dislike for Prussians and all things Prussian. One evening, I was returning to Munich in my car and stopped at a roadside *Gaststätte* (restaurant or tavern) in whose parking lot were a large number of long-distance trucks. I parked, entered the Gaststätte, and found it crowded with Bavarian truck drivers, who, judging by their loud talk, laughter, and singing, had been drinking beer for hours. At one table sat a huge Bavarian trucker with arms as thick as my legs and several other truckers of similar bulk. Each had an enormous stein of beer before him.

I thought of turning around to leave, but the bartender shouted, "*Guten Abend*" (Good evening), to me over the din. I walked to the bar and said in my best German, "*Ein Helles, bitte*" (a lager, please). The huge trucker noticed my accent and, half rising from his seat, asked in a loud and threatening voice, "*Sind Sie Preusse?*" (Are you a Prussian?)

It seemed to me that the room grew suddenly silent and that all eyes turned to me and the huge trucker. I replied, "*Nein, ich bin Amerikaner*" (No, I am an American).

A smile broke out on the trucker's face. He raised his stein and said to me . . . and to all others in the room, "*Sehr gut! Ein Prosit!*" (Very good! A toast!)

And so there was a happy ending because, *Gott sei dank* (thank God), I was not a Preusse.

Die Karte Muss Gestempelt Werden

We in the United States are familiar with bureaucracy. We think we invented it. But the Germans are at least our equals in this regard, and among the German bureaucracies none surpasses the police for sheer make-work.

One night in the spring of 1955, I was driving home in my assigned black Mercedes when I was stopped at a roadblock set up by the Munich police. I was waved over to the side of the road by a uniformed policeman and directed to the end of a line of cars awaiting attention by one or more of the several police officers present. I waited several minutes until my turn came and two police officers, each carrying a giant flashlight, approached my car. I rolled down the window beside me so I could talk with the officers. One of them came to my window and said in a polite but firm tone of command, "*Ihre Papiere, bitte*" (Your papers, please).

I handed him my American driver's license, my U.S. Army–issued driver's license, and a card from the glove compartment, signed by the Skipper as the Munich representative of COMNAVGER, that stated in English that I was authorized to use this car. The officer who took my papers flashed his light on them, examined them front and back, and appeared to be reading them. Calling the other officer to join him, he took the papers to the front of the car and examined them very carefully by the light of one of my headlights, handing each in turn to his colleague, who examined them and flashed his light on the car's license plate. They spoke briefly and quietly together, apparently concerned that my car, though officially a Navy car, was a German model with German civilian plates, not U.S. armed forces or diplomatic plates. After further discussion and turning the card over several times, they appeared to reach agreement on what to do.

Returning to my car window, one of the officers gave me back my driver's licenses but held the authorization card up for me to see and, pointing a flashlight at it, said in a serious tone, "Diese Karte passt nicht. Sie ist nicht gestempelt. Die Karte muss gestempelt werden." (This card is not sufficient. It is not stamped. The card must be stamped.) With that I was given the card and told to get it properly stamped and bring it to a certain *Polizeidienststelle* (police station) for approval.

The next morning I told the Skipper about the event. He laughed and said that the card did not look official enough to meet German police standards because, unlike important German documents, it bore no stamps or seals. "Get Joe to dress it up with stamps or seals. Use whatever we have that looks official and important." Joe quickly complied, and we all enjoyed seeing the card grow in dignity as it was stamped, "For Official Use Only," "By direction, Commander, U.S. Naval Forces Germany," "Priority," "APO 108, c/o U.S. Consulate, Munich."

I took the card to the police station and explained to the sergeant on duty the instructions I had received about the card. With a serious expression on his face the sergeant took the card, examined it carefully, front and back, and handed it back to me with a smile, saying, "Alles gut. Die Karte ist jetzt gestempelt worden. Schönen Tag, Herr Leutnant." (Everything is fine. The card has been stamped. Have a good day, Lieutenant.)

14

VISITS TO DACHAU

Dachau is a small Bavarian city about ten miles north and slightly west of Munich. It is infamous throughout the world as the site of a Nazi concentration camp—home to political tyranny; cruelty to Nazi Party opponents, communists, Jews, gypsies, homosexuals and others; forced labor for thousands and mass murder through gas chambers and gunfire; and atrocities inflicted by medical experiments on prisoners.

Dachau, the first of Germany's concentration camps, was established in March 1933, only two months after Hitler was named chancellor of Germany. It was the model for dozens of other such camps to follow. The Dachau camp grew in the years of Nazi rule to hold thousands of prisoners and to administer thirty or more subcamps in which more than thirty thousand slave laborers were forced to work—often to their death—in the production of armaments for the German Wehrmacht. On April 16, 1945, as American forces approached, Dachau and its subcamps held about seventy thousand prisoners; about two hundred thousand had been incarcerated there since it opened in 1933, and many thousands had perished there.[1] The administration of Dachau and other concentration camps was assigned to the police, who were required to join the Nazi Party, and to the SS (Schutzstaffel, the Nazi Party's paramilitary militia).

Naturally I was curious about the infamous concentration camp at Dachau and wanted to see it. One day Joe volunteered to drive me out to see the camp. It was a cold, windy day, with spurts of snow or cold rain falling from time to time. We parked near the entrance to

---

1. U.S. Holocaust Museum, "Dachau," Jewish Virtual Library, 2007, www.jewishvirtuallibrary.org/jsource/Holocaust/dachau.html.

the camp and walked in as far as was allowed at that time. There were electrified barbed wire fences twenty or thirty feet high, with guard towers at intervals, gray barracks, and buildings housing gas chambers for mass murders and crematoriums for corpse disposal. The sight was so horrible, so depressing, that I could not stay long before returning to the car.

On the way back to Munich, Joe told me that he had taken our Hausmeister, Herr Staudinger, at his request, to see the camp. "It was a tense and emotional trip," Joe said. "Between my little German and his broken English, we managed to communicate well enough while going to Dachau. As we sighted the camp entrance Staudinger grew quiet. We walked slowly through the grounds, saw the barbed wire fences and towers, the barracks, the gas chambers, and the crematorium ovens. There were some signs and explanations around the camp in German, and he read them. Finally, after seeing the crematorium, Staudinger turned to me and said, '*Geh' ma*' [in Bavarian dialect, Let's go]. He had tears in his eyes; he was crying and struggling to gain control of himself.

"On the way back to Munich, Staudinger was mostly silent, but he sobbed softly from time to time and spoke quietly. He said that he had been in Munich all during the war but had heard nothing about the camp at Dachau. After the war he heard bits of information but avoided thinking of it, trying not to believe the stories he heard. But now he had seen that the stories were true."

Joe took a deep breath and continued: "He knew also that the camps were run by the police and SS, that the police were required to join the Nazi Party to keep their jobs, and that some of them joined the SS. Herr Staudinger knew that Herr Schnabel, our guard at Possart Platz 3, was a retired Munich policeman who had been in the police throughout the war."

Joe took another deep breath and finished his story: "After our visit to Dachau, Herr Staudinger would not speak with Herr Schnabel."

PART 3

GERMANY TRANSFORMED: ENEMY TO ALLY

15

THE GEHLEN ORGANIZATION: REINHARD GEHLEN AND JAMES CRITCHFIELD

Origins of Gehlen Organization

In August 1945, only three months after Germany surrendered unconditionally, Gen. Reinhard Gehlen, chief of Germany's military intelligence organization aimed at the Soviets—the General Staff's Fremde Heere Ost (Foreign Armies East or FHO)—and a small group of his officers, constituting the core of FHO, were secretly removed from their POW camps by the U.S. Army European Command and flown to the United States in the personal airplane of Gen. Dwight Eisenhower's chief of staff, Gen. Bedell Smith. FHO's key files on the Russian armed forces also went to Washington. Gehlen and his group were held and interrogated for about a year at Fort Hunt, Virginia, a secret Army interrogation center, whose cover name was Post Office Box 1152.

About a year later, in July 1946, the U.S. Army secretly brought Gehlen, his assistants, and the FHO files back to Germany to create a new super secret German intelligence organization—the Gehlen Organization—directed to obtain for the United States urgently needed information about the Soviet armed forces and intentions. The Gehlen Organization grew rapidly to several thousand persons, including many former German armed forces officers, especially former General Staff officers. After several moves the organization was established in a secluded walled compound in Pullach, near Munich.

In 1949 responsibility for the organization was transferred from the U.S. Army to the newly created U.S. Central Intelligence Agency (CIA). The CIA supported and supervised the Gehlen Organization for about eight years, until, in 1956, the organization was taken over by the government of the new democratic West Germany as its own foreign intelligence agency, the *Bundesnachrichtendienst* (Federal

Intelligence Service or BND). The BND still operates today, with its main base still in Pullach, offices in many German cities, and agents in many countries.

Those are the bare facts. They raise many questions, and they hide as much as they reveal. Were General Gehlen or other German officers who were taken into the organization Nazis? Had they committed, authorized, or otherwise been involved in any of the war crimes committed by Nazi Germany? Why would the United States support its former enemies to spy on its wartime ally, the USSR?

The Gehlen Organization was conceived in deepest secrecy and has operated in secrecy ever since. Even today, sixty years after its establishment, very few Americans know of its existence as the German intelligence service and still fewer know anything of its history or its significance in the Cold War and its role in Germany's transformation from enemy to ally.

Gen. Reinhard Gehlen and Fremde Heere Ost

Gen. Reinhard Gehlen is at the center of the Gehlen Organization's story. He was born in Erfurt, Germany, in 1902, completed his secondary education in 1920 at age eighteen, and joined the German Army that same year. He became an officer, performed well in a variety of posts over a period of years, attended staff college from 1933 to 1935, and became a member of the elite German Army General Staff in 1935 when he was thirty-three. At the outbreak of the war on September 1, 1939, he was serving in the fortifications branch of the General Staff, but by 1940 he had been moved to the Western Front, where he served in a variety of positions, ending as liaison officer to Gen. Heinz Guderian's Panzer Group during the blitzkrieg attack on France.

When French resistance collapsed in June 1940, Gehlen was named adjutant to Gen. Franz Halder, chief of the General Staff, and then chief of the Eastern Group of the General Staff's operations branch. Finally, on April 1, 1942, he was appointed head of Fremde Heere Ost, the General Staff's intelligence branch for the East Front. He served as chief of FHO for about three years, until April 1945.

Gehlen's task in his FHO intelligence post was not easy. Arriving in April 1942, he was just in time to witness and report on the high-water mark of the German invasion of Russia but then had to report and evaluate the defeats that followed. When the German attack on Russia was launched on June 22, 1941, Hitler and many high-ranking

German officers thought that the German Army would smash Russian resistance and overthrow Stalin's Communist government in a matter of weeks. The German forces achieved great victories in 1941, but they were stopped at the gates of Leningrad and Moscow and forced to endure the bitterly cold Russian winter of 1941–42 in the field. When spring came in 1942, the German armies went back on the offensive, but Hitler changed his priorities and shifted some forces from the attack on Moscow to strengthen a drive to take the industrial areas of Stalingrad and Kharkov. At Stalingrad the German armies again failed to destroy the Russian defenders and were forced to pass a second winter in the field. The battle for Stalingrad continued through that winter of 1942–43 and ended with the surrender of the half-starved, freezing, and wounded German Sixth Army, which was attacking the city—and the turn of the tide of battle on Germany's East Front.

In the summer of 1943 at the giant Battle of Kursk, the Soviet army defeated the Germans and went on to take back a great part of what the Germans had occupied since the war began. Casualties were very high on both sides, but this was worse for the Germans for they had run out of reserves of men and matériel, while the Soviets grew stronger.

Gehlen described the events on the East Front accurately in daily reports to Hitler, but the Führer, growing increasingly irrational, refused to believe bad news and increasingly distrusted the bearers. The Führer rejected Gehlen's reports and dismissed him from his daily briefings. Gehlen's reports were, however, included in the daily briefings by Gen. Heinz Guderian, whom Hitler had appointed chief of the General Staff.

The year 1944 was even worse for the Germans than 1943 had been. In June 1944 the Western Allies successfully landed in Normandy, enlarged their bridgeheads, and swept across France, advancing toward the Rhine. The Russian armies drove the Germans back westward until by the end of the year the Soviet forces had reached the Oder River, only a short distance from Berlin. And to top it all, in July 1944 some officers of the General Staff had attempted to assassinate Hitler. After the bomb plot, Hitler trusted his generals less and less. Neither General Guderian nor General Gehlen participated in the bomb plot, but the paranoia it instilled in Hitler added to his rejection of their reports.

Guderian and Gehlen continued to report accurately the enemy advances on the East Front and Hitler's distrust of them grew. On March 28, 1945, Hitler dismissed General Guderian from his position as chief of the General Staff and on April 9, 1945, the Führer sent written notice of dismissal to General Gehlen. Both were in considerable danger of arrest on Hitler's orders.

Gehlen's Plan

Noting Hitler's refusal to believe the truth about Germany's desperate situation, General Gehlen began a series of clandestine meetings with trusted FHO officers to develop a plan to align Germany with the Western Allies to protect the long-term interests of the German people.

Gehlen and his colleagues were practical men. They knew that the Soviet armies were advancing from the east with increasing forces and speed. The British, American, Free French and Allied forces had broken out of their landing areas on the Normandy beaches and were sweeping eastward across France to the Rhine. Other armies of the Western Allies had taken Sicily and most of Italy. British and American bombers were systematically destroying German cities and Germany's transportation infrastructure. In short, General Gehlen and his colleagues saw that the war was lost.

Gehlen was convinced that the British, French, and Americans had interests and goals contrary to those of the Soviets and that there would soon be a falling out between the Russians and the Western Allies. Gehlen further believed that Germany would be free and sovereign again some day and that he and his colleagues could help protect the present German people from Russian captivity and help create the new Germany by reaching an agreement with the Western powers. And Gehlen had something to offer: the German Army— through the FHO's work—had the best information outside the Soviet Union on the Soviet forces, their manpower, their equipment, their tactics, and their intentions, and it had a network of sources in Eastern Europe.

To advance his plan, Gehlen had copies made of FHO's most valuable intelligence files and hid them in safe places known only to a few persons of his group. One set of the files, for example, was hidden in abandoned salt mines of the Bavarian Alps.

On April 28, 1945, Gehlen and several of his fellow officers of FHO went into hiding at a remote and uninhabited mountain lodge called Elendsalm in the Bavarian Alps. They planned to wait there until they could surrender to the American Army and propose to the Americans that they renew the German intelligence effort against the Soviets, for the benefit of the United States and the interests of a future Germany. Gehlen offered to reassemble the best of his FHO officers, reawaken FHO's network of informants, and turn over the entire intelligence output to the United States. In return, he proposed that the United States equip and support his secretly reconstituted intelligence organization and not ask it to do anything contrary to the interests of a future free Germany.

The plan was easy to make but hard to carry out. The United States had been at war with Germany on land, in the air, and at sea since 1941. Hundreds of thousands of American soldiers, airmen, sailors, and merchant seamen had been killed or wounded. The giant and bloody Battle of the Bulge and the infamous Malmedy Massacre, during which a German SS commander executed American prisoners of war, had occurred only months before. U.S. and British troops fighting their way into Germany had just discovered the death camps of the Holocaust. From General Eisenhower to Private GI Joe, American soldiers were bitterly angry with their German foe, in a mood to try German generals as war criminals, not to join with them against America's Soviet ally. The American public shared this revulsion against the Germans and would probably disapprove of treating a group of General Staff officers as allies instead of as prisoners of war and possibly war criminals.

Gehlen's Surrender

Early in May 1945 the American army entered Bavaria and received the surrender of thousands of German soldiers. On May 22, 1945, Gehlen led his colleagues, in uniform, down from their hideout at Elendsalm with the intention of surrendering to the American army and presenting his plan to the American authorities. Things did not work out as simply as he hoped. General Gehlen surrendered in the town hall of the small Bavarian town of Fischhausen; he, a brigadier general of the German Army, and member of its General Staff found in the town hall only a young American soldier who spoke no German and didn't understand a word that Gehlen said.[1] He and his colleagues were treated the same as thousands of others; they were treated

---

1. Mary Ellen Reese, *General Reinhard Gehlen: The CIA Connection* (Fairfax, VA: George Mason University Press, 1990), 40.

respectfully, disarmed, and sent to POW camps, with all the rights of prisoners of war.

I've heard a different version of General Gehlen's surrender that is perhaps apocryphal but fitting and more humorous and memorable than the one just mentioned. As I heard the story in Munich in 1955, General Gehlen and his group, along with other surrendering German soldiers, waited in the small town for an approaching column of American tanks. The tank column stopped. General Gehlen stepped out in front of his colleagues and saluted the lead tank's commander, a sergeant whose head and shoulders rose out of the tank. Gehlen said, in German-accented English, "I am General Reinhard Gehlen of the General Staff, chief of military intelligence on the East Front."

"Yeah, and I am Jesus Christ," replied the tank sergeant, who pointed to the other surrendering soldiers and said, "Get in line over there with the others."

Gehlen and Colleagues as Prisoners of War

By the last days of April, Russian troops had reached Berlin and were fighting their way into the city center to capture the Reichstag and Hitler's chancellery. On April 30, 1945, Hitler committed suicide to avoid capture. He had named ADM Karl Dönitz as his successor and ordered the shift of the government to Flensburg, near the border with Denmark.

British, American, and Soviet forces rushed to take Flensburg, and so great was the mistrust between the Western Allies and the Russians that shooting broke out temporarily between them, with the Germans in the crossfire. Unable to agree, each side established its own supervisory commission to organize German demobilization, including the finding and arrest of high-ranking German officers.

Gehlen and his colleagues immediately became top priority targets of both sides, and a race was on to find them. Gehlen and his group were, of course, in the American zone and soon were prisoners of war of the United States. Gehlen was separated from his group and sent to Wörgl, near the ski resort of Kitzbühel in Austria; then he was moved to the Army Counterintelligence Center at Salzburg, then to Augsburg, and finally to a prison in Wiesbaden. At each stop he was interrogated by a higher and higher U.S. Army authority, none of whom showed any interest in or gave any encouragement to his plan. It is possible, however, that his frequent moves and the Army's backlog of paperwork kept his whereabouts unknown to the supervisory commissions who were looking for him and might have saved him from the violence or even death that he would have endured were he turned over to the Soviet commission.

Finally, Gehlen's luck changed. The British and American supervisory commissions at Flensburg learned about Gehlen and the FHO from an interrogation of one of his former staff and signaled Wiesbaden to be on the alert for his possible arrival there. Army Counterintelligence in Wiesbaden turned over the information about Gehlen and FHO to Gen. Edwin Sibert, chief of intelligence for the Twelfth Army Group, who had a keen interest in information about the Soviet Union and its forces. Fortune smiled on Gehlen again; his interrogation was assigned to a young American army officer, Capt. John Boker, who spoke fluent German and had considerable background in German military matters and the Soviet Union from earlier interrogations of German officers who had fought on the East Front. Captain Boker already had grave concerns about Soviet aggressive intentions. He treated General Gehlen with courtesy and quickly won his confidence. Gehlen was moved from the prison to a villa in Wiesbaden, which formed part of an Army interrogation center. Boker's research and conversations with Gehlen satisfied him that Gehlen was not a Nazi; that his loyalties ran to the German nation, its Wehrmacht, and especially its General Staff, not to the Nazi Party; and that his group might bring valuable intelligence about the Soviet forces. General Sibert agreed. With the support of General Sibert, Boker tracked down Gehlen's FHO colleagues in their various POW camps, brought them together again with Gehlen at Wiesbaden and retrieved the hidden FHO files—all in utmost secrecy. Gehlen was still a wanted man sought by both the British and the Soviets. To protect him, Boker arranged to have Gehlen's name removed from the list of prisoners of war in U.S. custody.

The Gehlen Group Is Flown to the United States for Interrogation

In late August 1945, only three months after Gehlen's surrender, Gehlen, his group of FHO officers, and the FHO files disappeared. The Army secretly loaded them and Captain Boker into the personal plane of Gen. Bedell Smith, chief of staff to General Eisenhower, and flew them across the Atlantic to Washington, D.C. They then were taken in a windowless van to Post Office Box 1152, the secret intelligence interrogation center at Fort Hunt, near Alexandria, Virginia.

Gehlen and his colleagues were held at Post Office Box 1152 for about eleven months—eleven months of interrogations, monitoring, work on intelligence tasks concerning the Soviet Union to test their knowledge and abilities, and eleven months of uncertainty about their future. While some considered the Germans to be cooperating experts with badly needed information and potential to get much more, others saw them as enemy prisoners of war. There were inevitable struggles for control: the Pentagon versus the U.S. European Command and the authorities running Fort Hunt versus those specially assigned to the Gehlen project.

Captain Boker was relieved of his liaison position and assigned other duties but managed to stay in touch with the project. Fortune was still with Gehlen and his officers, however, as another German-speaking U.S. Army captain experienced in interrogations, Eric Waldman, was placed in charge. Captain Waldman, like Captain Boker, concluded after investigation that Gehlen was not a Nazi or Nazi sympathizer and that his proposal deserved consideration. Captain Waldman fought hard for his wards and won victories to get them out of the prisonlike cells in which the Fort Hunt authorities had placed them and move them to more comfortable quarters.

Waldman treated the Germans with courtesy, won their respect and even their friendship. Even so, it was not at all a sure thing that U.S. Army support for a German intelligence agency run by a German general would be approved in the climate of 1945–46, not at all clear that one German general and his group of General Staff officers would be hired to spy on our Soviet wartime ally while other high-ranking German officers and officials were on trial for war crimes in Nuremberg.

The Cold War Escalates

The Gehlen project was, however, secretly approved in 1946. In fact, the Soviets' own hostile acts in Europe and elsewhere changed the climate of opinion and brought about the approval. The Americans and the British began rapidly demobilizing their armies in Europe at the end of the war, but the Soviet Union maintained large armies menacing the West. The Soviets were confrontational, not cooperative, in efforts to solve problems of the occupation in Germany. There were a series of communist coups in Eastern Europe and large communist demonstrations in Italy and France. In January 1946 Soviet forces occupied Manchuria and entered North Korea. In March 1946 they massed troops on the Turkish border and, contrary to an agreement, refused to withdraw their troops from Iran.

The rapid escalation of tensions led Winston Churchill to sound a warning in his famous "Iron Curtain" speech in March 1946. In the spring and summer of 1946 tensions ran so high that some even thought that war with the Soviets was possible. American military commanders viewed the situation as fraught with danger. They had, except for the military police, only two divisions in Europe. The Soviets, by contrast, had many more divisions, many more tanks, many more guns and rocket launchers—but how many more? One hundred divisions? Two hundred divisions? And where were they placed? And how supplied? The U.S. Army had no reliable information to answer such questions and to monitor the changes. In this new climate Gehlen's group offered what the Army wanted most, expertise about the Soviet Union, its capabilities, its intentions, and the order of battle of its forces in Europe.

The Gehlen Group Returns

In July 1946, in complete secrecy, the U.S. Army returned Gehlen and his group to Germany. Eric Waldman had gone before them to make necessary arrangements. They were housed in comfortable quarters at Oberursel, a U.S. Army interrogation center. Their families were allowed to join them, but secrecy and security provisions were strictly enforced.

The U.S. Army and Gehlen must have made official an agreement or plan before the Germans left Fort Hunt, but according to General Gehlen, he and General Sibert, who was still in charge of all U.S. Army intelligence in Germany, made only an oral agreement, sealed with a handshake. Gehlen wrote that the gist of the agreement was:

- General Gehlen would reassemble the best of his FHO staff and create a German intelligence agency whose entire output would be provided to the U.S. Army and whose focus would be on the Soviet bloc;
- The U.S. Army would support the Gehlen Organization financially and with supplies and some equipment;
- The Gehlen Organization would not be required to work against the interests of a future Germany; and
- The arrangement would continue until Germany was again a

sovereign state, and the organization would then be offered to the new German state.[2]

The Gehlen Organization Is Launched

After Gehlen's return to Germany, the organization was launched quickly. Lt. Col. John Russell Deane Jr. was placed in overall charge of the effort by Gen. Lucius Clay, the head of the U.S. military government in Germany. Deane did not speak German, so dealing directly with the Germans was left to Captain Waldman, who was still assigned to the project. Deane handled matters of policy; Waldman, day-to-day implementation.

The organization grew rapidly as it reassembled former FHO officers and other former German officers, especially General Staff officers, who had access to German political, business, and former military circles.

Money was a critical problem because the U.S. Army had no specific authorization from Congress to create a German intelligence agency and no appropriated funds to support it. The solution reached was both ingenious and effective. The Army gave the organization a monopoly of the black market for cigarettes in the American zone. The Army provided the cigarettes, special units of the Gehlen Organization sold them on the black market at prices far higher than the price at the Army PX, and often the Army Criminal Affairs Division caught the buyers and repossessed the cigarettes. Large sums were raised but considerable friction arose between the American military and local German police authorities not privy to the secret organization and doing their duty to prevent black marketing. It was particularly galling to the American and German law enforcement units when a Gehlen agent involved in the cigarette trade was arrested only to be released on orders from higher authority.

Move to Pullach

The organization went right to work, opening offices in a number of West German cities, contacting former FHO agents in the Soviet bloc, recruiting new sources, and sending new agents into the Soviet bloc.

---

2. Reinhard Gehlen, *The Service: The Memoirs of General Reinhard Gehlen*, trans. David Irving (New York: World Publishing, 1972), 121. A longer and perhaps self-serving description of the terms of the reported oral agreement can be found on page 122 of Gehlen's memoir.

By mid-1947 the organization's headquarters at Oberursel was badly overcrowded, and new quarters were found for it at Pullach, near to Munich. The new quarters were almost ideal—a secluded location, a gated compound surrounded by high walls enclosing many acres, with a large central house, twenty or so family-sized houses, roads, a club-house, a number of barracks, a mess hall, a garage, and a swimming pool. For security reasons, top German staff were required to bring their families to live with them in the compound. After the organization moved in, it added a school, a kindergarten, and a small PX. The compound had a significant Nazi history as the headquarters of Martin Bormann, Hitler's trusted lieutenant.

The organization was producing many intelligence reports on the Soviet bloc. It remained, however, quite controversial in the small circle of American intelligence officers who knew of its existence. Things were changing, however, in favor of Gehlen's project. President Harry Truman had dissolved the wartime Office of Strategic Services in 1945 and created a Central Intelligence Group to coordinate among the military and other intelligence agencies. In 1947 the National Security Act was enacted, which, among other things, established the Central Intelligence Agency, which was given responsibility for American clandestine or covert activities abroad. The Central Intelligence Agency and U.S. military intelligence agencies were uncertain about the future of General Gehlen's organization.

The CIA Replaces the U.S. Army as the Gehlen Organization's Sponsor

In 1948 the Army and CIA agreed to a joint study of the Gehlen Organization, a study conducted primarily by a young former Army colonel, James Critchfield, who had left his Army career to become a CIA officer. Critchfield found the Gehlen Organization to be already so large—a German staff of several thousand people—and so active that it was too late to take minor measures about it. In his opinion, U.S. Army intelligence was supporting the Gehlen Organization but not sufficiently monitoring or controlling it. He suggested that the United States had only two choices: it could eliminate the Gehlen Organization or get closely involved and try to control it. The CIA decided to take over the Army's role and to improve support and supervision.

The CIA named James Critchfield to be chief of the CIA project concerning the Gehlen Organization and assembled a group of seven

CIA officers for the task. In July 1949 the CIA team, operating under military cover (i.e., each acting as an American military officer) and led by Critchfield, back in uniform as a colonel, took command. Critchfield placed the CIA offices in the big house—the Bormann house—of the compound, a nonverbal but explicit statement of his intention to assert control.

A security rule of the organization at that time required that all staff use cover names. James Critchfield was "Kent J. Marshall"; General Gehlen was "Doktor Schneider." These names were still in use during my time in Munich.

The Gehlen Organization Becomes the Federal Intelligence Service

The CIA–Gehlen Organization combination operated from July 1949 until the Gehlen Organization was taken over and made part of the government of the newly sovereign Federal Republic of Germany in 1956. It was renamed the Bundesnachrictendienst (Federal Intelligence Service) and thus became West Germany's foreign intelligence service. General Gehlen remained at its head until his retirement on April 30, 1968.[3] He died on June 9, 1979, at age seventy-seven.

The years 1946 to 1956 were the formative years of the Gehlen Organization, years in which it was a major actor in the Cold War and won the respect and favor of the West German chancellor and parliament. It had its victories and its defeats. Its agents in the East kept up a steady stream of reporting on the USSR, Poland, East Germany, and other Soviet bloc nations. In return it was penetrated by Soviet and East German intelligence organizations[4] and continued to be the target of a super secret campaign by the U.S. Army Counterintelligence Corps (CIC), a campaign unknown even to the CIA.[5] The American-German cooperative intelligence activities through the Gehlen Organization are important in the history of Europe and the Cold War, but much about this partnership is unknown by the public even today.

By the time I arrived in Munich in 1955, the Gehlen Organization had grown to include several thousand people. While supported by

---

3. Gehlen, *The Service*, 380.
4. Reese, *General Reinhard Gehlen*, 143–171; Gehlen, *The Service*, 243–252.
5. Reese, *General Reinhard Gehlen*, 132–141.

the U.S. Army or CIA, it directed its efforts almost entirely at intelligence about the Soviet bloc (or at least that was supposed to be the case). After its absorption by the West German government in 1956, it was frequently tasked to supply information about other areas and rather quickly became a service covering the whole world, with contacts and agents in many countries.

My contacts were with the Navy section of the Evaluation Branch; I had no contact with the organization's intelligence collection operations, except, of course, for receiving its products. I have read or heard, however, of some important and colorful operations showing the professionalism of its efforts. For example, James Critchfield, in his book *Partners at the Creation*, writes about a Gehlen Organization radio monitoring station near Wiesbaden manned by about ten German radio intercept operators whom he visited during the Berlin Blockade. The experienced German intercept operators, using equipment in part supplied by the American forces at Wiesbaden, monitored all Soviet air and ground voice radio traffic in East Germany, tracking in real time whether the Soviet MIGs were up or down, in what numbers, and which fields were in use. In addition other Gehlen agents on the ground in East Germany were locating and watching all Soviet airfields, counting the MIGs on the ground, and rapidly reporting numbers and movements. These intelligence operations were important to the success of the Berlin Airlift.[6] The Baltic Fishery Protection Service was the cover name for a Gehlen Organization operation carried out in cooperation with the British Secret Intelligence Service (MI-6) and the Royal Navy. This daring operation will be further described in the next chapter. In addition, numerous operations collected the information I received in reports about the Soviet and Polish navies, the Baltic, the Barents and White Sea ports, the Danube River traffic, and of course, the East German railroad traffic.

I heard stories of two other operations, but I cannot verify them: I was told that the Gehlen Organization secretly made contact with the Spanish intelligence service and was allowed to establish a radio monitoring facility along Spain's Mediterranean coast that was capable of intercepting radio traffic in the Mediterranean Sea, including the radio traffic of the American Sixth Fleet. If true, it reminds us that

---

6. James H. Critchfield, *Partners at the Creation: The Men Behind Postwar Germany's Defense and Intelligence Establishments* (Annapolis, MD: Naval Institute Press, 2003), 86–87.

despite all assurances to the contrary, national interests still govern the actions of intelligence agencies of our allies as well as our enemies. According to another story, the Gehlen Organization made an effort to exploit a visit by a flotilla of Soviet Navy ships to North German ports by making it easy for Soviet sailors to defect, if they were so inclined. As told to me, the Gehlen Organization recruited "ladies of the evening" from all over Europe to be sure to cover all the bars, restaurants, and nightspots where Soviet sailors on liberty ashore might stop. These ladies were to entice the sailors to stay and offer help to sailors who might want to escape to the West. There was also talk of fake disease outbreaks and quarantines to keep the Soviet sailors ashore.

James H. Critchfield, Val Rychly's CIA Connection

James H. Critchfield was the CIA's chief of the project for support of the Gehlen Organization from 1949 to 1956. From his great success in Germany, Critchfield went on to a number of other CIA responsibilities and served for a number of years as chief of the CIA's Near East division.

Critchfield, a U.S. Army colonel, had commanded a tank battalion in the invasion of southern France during World War II. Landing at the beach at Frejus on the famed French Riviera, his battalion fought its way northward across southeast France, into Germany, and down into Bavaria and Austria. As the fighting ended he was assigned to Vienna on the intelligence staff of the U.S. Army general in command of U.S. forces in occupied Austria and was appointed head of U.S. operational intelligence activities in Austria. According to Critchfield, he first met Val Rychly in about 1946 when Rychly, then a naval attaché in Prague and Belgrade, was traveling widely in Czechoslovakia and the Balkans. Rychly frequently stopped to meet with Critchfield in Vienna to exchange information about and interpret events in these countries. In those visits they became good friends.

I met Critchfield only once during my service in Munich and heard of his whereabouts thereafter from the Skipper. The relationship between Val Rychly and Jim Critchfield was close. While I was in Munich I understood that they were working together in some fashion and for some object, but it was all very secret and never explained to me. Even though on two occasions I served as a courier to deliver packages from the Skipper to Critchfield, I knew nothing about the packages' contents.

My first courier mission was to deliver a package to Critchfield at his office in the Bormann house in the Pullach compound. I wore my uniform, showed my ID to the guards at the gate, and, following directions given me by the Skipper, drove straight to the Bormann house. I parked in front of the house, entered the big front door, crossed a large empty foyer, and mounted an elegant stairway to Critchfield's second-floor office. I walked to his secretary's desk, and following my instructions, said, "Good morning. I am Lieutenant JG Marvin Durning," and handing the package to her, "Commander Rychly asked me to deliver this to Mr. Marshall."

She smiled, took the package, and asked me to be seated for a minute while she delivered it. She went into the office behind her, and to my surprise but great pleasure, Critchfield himself came out. I stood up at once to acknowledge his friendly greeting, "Hello, Mr. Durning, Val Rychly has told us of you, and I am pleased to meet you in person. Thank you for the package. My best wishes to Commander Rychly." With that he turned to reenter his office as I said, "Thank you, Sir." Our meeting took about one minute and was the only time I saw James Critchfield until many years later.

My second occasion to deliver a package from the Skipper to Critchfield via his secretary came several months later. Following careful instructions, I again wore my uniform and this time drove to McGraw Kaserne and, within this fortress, to the grocery portion of the Army Post Exchange. I found a parking space and at the appointed time entered the supermarket, carrying my package in my right hand. I took a shopping cart and pushed it slowly past several aisles and entered a designated aisle at the end of which I saw Critchfield's secretary, who was examining a shelf of canned goods. No one else was in the aisle so I pushed my cart toward her as she pushed hers toward me. As we met, I dropped my package quickly into the basket of her cart, among the vegetables and canned goods. She said nothing but glanced very briefly at me in acknowledgement of receipt and, pushing on past me, continued her shopping. I bought a few things because an empty cart might attract attention at the checkout line, went through the checkout line, walked back to my car, and drove back to Possart Platz 3. She and I said nothing to each other during the brief moment when we passed in the aisle; it was unnecessary, for we recognized each other and everything happened exactly as planned.

Years later, in the late 1970s when we were both living in Washington, D.C., I again met James Critchfield. He invited me to the offices of his engineering firm in a Washington suburb. His offices were in one of the modern buildings on the Virginia side of the Potomac. His receptionist called him on my arrival, and he came out to meet me. He said he had arranged for me to meet his staff. We went to a conference room with a large table and chairs around it sufficient for perhaps twenty people. The walls of the room were covered with topographic maps. He explained that they were maps of the Sultanate of Oman and that his firm was working on the water problems of this Gulf state. They seemed to me to be expert in and truly concerned about the water problems, but I could not see Jim Critchfield as totally absent from the field of intelligence in Near Eastern affairs. He had so much experience, so many skills and talents, that it was unlikely he would be completely separated from intelligence work.

This meeting with Critchfield was interesting, and I was flattered that he remembered me, took the time to meet with me, and introduced me to his staff. He later told me he was "devoted to Val Rychly." I regret that I cannot tell more about their cooperative work, but I know no more—I had no need to know. It may seem strange that I could feel so comfortable with Jim Critchfield even though I had seen him so little, but I did. I felt I was privileged to be a member of a team—a Rychly-Critchfield team, a Navy-CIA team—that had done important work.

16

THE ADMIRALS AND THE NEW GERMAN NAVY

I arrived in Munich in time to witness and participate in the drama of the creation of a new, sovereign, and democratic West Germany that would be recognized by the Western Allies, be rearmed, and join the North Atlantic Treaty Organization (NATO) alliance. The key players of the intelligence and naval portions of this drama had all been at work toward these goals since 1948 or earlier. To recap, when I arrived,

- Val Rychly was in charge at the U.S. Navy's intelligence office at Possart Platz 3, which comprised one or two U.S. Navy officers, several yeomen, and a small German staff. Rychly received in person German-language copies of all Gehlen Organization reports on matters of interest to the U.S. Navy.
- The Gehlen Organization was headquartered in its compound in Pullach and had regional and local offices throughout West Germany and "residents" in foreign countries of special interest. It had grown into an organization of several thousand employees and would be absorbed into the Bundesrepublik government as its foreign intelligence agency.
- James Critchfield and his staff of CIA officers were at Pullach supporting and monitoring the Gehlen Organization and receiving its intelligence products.
- The U.S. Army was still a large presence in the city. The headquarters of the Seventh Army was in McGraw Kaserne, and the Army's Intelligence and Counterintelligence Corps (CIC) were active throughout the former American occupation zone.

The years 1955 and 1956 were times of fundamental change in

Germany. The Paris Agreements signed on October 23, 1954, by the Federal Republic, the United States, Britain, and France provided for restoration of full sovereignty to the Federal Republic and its acceptance into NATO. These provisions were to take effect fully on May 5, 1955. Implementation would require several more years.

Mysterious Visitors

I had been in Munich only a few weeks when the first of several mysterious German visitors—a man of about fifty in a well-tailored business suit, with an erect, military bearing—came to our offices. He walked upstairs with the Skipper, said hello to Joe, and disappeared into the Skipper's office. The door was shut behind him, and remained closed for an hour or more, at which point the man and the Skipper left together. I was working at my desk with the door to my office open, so I caught glimpses of the visitor for a few moments as he arrived and as he departed. The Skipper did not introduce me. I had no idea who the visitor was, but I surmised that he was important. It was very unusual for visitors to be allowed on the second floor and especially rare for them to be permitted to enter the Skipper's office, the sanctum sanctorum of Possart Platz 3. Joe offered no explanation, and I knew better than to ask.

From time to time other German visitors—all middle-aged men in business suits, usually carrying briefcases—would arrive and the scenario would be repeated. Once I overheard the Skipper ask Joe to drive his visitor to the train station in one of the Navy cars.

Reports of the Admirals' Meetings

About two months after my arrival, the mystery of the German visitors was explained. One morning, shortly after Frau Raab had served coffee, Joe appeared at my office door and said that the Skipper would like to see me. I walked the few steps across the foyer where the yeomen had their desks and entered the Skipper's office. He was sitting at his desk looking dead tired, as if he hadn't slept at all the night before. Joe followed me, holding some typewritten pages in his hand.

"I'd like you to help me with an important matter, one which we have not yet discussed. You have undoubtedly noticed my occasional German visitors and wondered about them," said the Skipper. "You have not asked, and I appreciate that, but it is time now for you to know about them and to help me. In this office only the three of us— you, Joe, and I—are cleared to participate in this activity. Everything about it—even the fact that the activity exists—is secret. We send our reports to the director of Naval Intelligence in Washington, but not through Berlin or Heidelberg or any other chain of command.

"The visitors you have seen are former admirals of Germany's World War II Navy, the Kriegsmarine. There are four of them. I meet with them regularly at my house. They are sponsored by and financially supported by the U.S. Navy. Sometimes they are called the Naval Historical Team [NHT], a name which was originally descriptive of some of their work, but is now a cover name, for their activities concern the future. They are making plans for a new German Navy and building support for it so that it can be launched soon, when Germany regains her sovereignty, rearms, and joins the NATO alliance. They meet frequently, in the privacy of my house, where they often stay well past midnight and sometimes for two or three days. We treat them well and give them the respect due admirals and appreciation for their current work for our common cause.

"No matter how late their meetings run, I stay up as long as necessary to dictate a report of what was said. I am very tired as I do this, and my dictation is often a garbled mixture of German and English. Sometimes it is impossible for Joe to transcribe. He has to wait for me to help and that's too slow. We must go faster.

"Joe has in his hand his attempted transcription of what I dictated last night and"—he handed me a dictation cassette—"here is my dictation tape. Please organize this report and edit it into good English. Give it to Joe to type. If you can't decipher something, ask me. These reports have top priority. When a report is ready, bring it to me. I'll review it, sign it, and send it on its way. And remember, these reports are secret."

With that he left to return to his house in the Gabriel Max Strasse for lunch with his guests, the admirals. Joe handed me the sheets of paper in his hand and, with a big friendly grin, said, "Congratulations, Mr. Durning. You have won the Skipper's trust. Now you get to work even more hours translating, rewriting, and editing the Skipper's late-night dictations."

Making clear sense of the dictation wasn't easy and often required many drafts. The Skipper was pleased with my work on the initial report, and thereafter, I edited all of his reports about the Naval Historical Team and their plans for the new German Navy.

Editing the Skipper's reports was like sitting in on the admirals' meetings. I often discussed the reports with the Skipper to make sure

I had them just right, and this allowed me more information and insight into the meetings' significance. The admirals were defining the missions, ships, yards, personnel, and tactics of the soon-to-be-formed Bundesmarine (Federal Navy). They were confidential advisers to Chancellor Konrad Adenauer and his civilian defense chief, Theodor Blank, head of the shadow ministry of defense in Bonn. In making their plans, the admirals necessarily stayed in contact with the chancellor, his aides, military and military-related committees of the parliament (the *Bundestag*), the leadership of the major parties, and the many German Navy veterans groups. The missions, bases, and fleet of the planned Navy would be part of the Western Alliance's strategy for the defense of Europe against Soviet attack. Like Chancellor Adenauer and the rest of West Germany's leadership, the admirals insisted that the Alliance be committed to a policy of strong defense of all of West Germany, not a strategy of fallback to the Rhine, or to the English Channel, or to the North Atlantic.

Although other former German officers had participated in the historical studies in the earlier years of the Naval Historical Team, only four were members of the group meeting at the Skipper's house at the time of my service in Munich: Adms. Konrad Patzig, Friedrich Ruge, Gerhard Wagner, and Helmuth Heye. All had served in high-ranking positions in the former German Navy. None had been a member of or sympathizer with the Nazi Party; none was charged with or suspected of commission of war crimes. All were respected by the former officers of the German Navy. I learned much about each of them by editing the Skipper's reports, more from conversations with the Skipper in the course of my editing, and some from books written in recent years.

Naturally, momentous issues like the return of sovereignty to and rearmament of Germany were negotiated at the highest levels (i.e., by the German chancellor, the American president, his secretary of state, and the prime ministers of Britain and France, together with their secretaries or ministers of foreign affairs and defense, and their aides). In this case, however, the diplomats followed paths paved in advance by secret intelligence agencies, especially the U.S. Army and the CIA, which established, supported, and supervised the Gehlen Organization, U.S. Naval Intelligence, and the former German admirals in the Naval Historical Team.

Early Postwar Steps toward the New German Navy

By 1948 the Cold War tensions between the Soviet Union and the

Western Allies had become acute. In 1948 the Soviets carried out a coup in Czechoslovakia and imposed the Berlin Blockade with the intention of driving the Western powers' armed forces out of Berlin. These aggressive or confrontational actions, together with others around the world, such as the establishment of communist governments in Eastern Europe without free elections, the communist insurgency in Greece, and the Soviets' refusal to withdraw troops from Iran, raised a critical alarm in the West. The Western Allies hardened their policies against the Soviet threats. Several projects, forerunners to the new German Navy, were carried out by former German Navy personnel under British or American sponsorship, namely, the Baltic Fishery Protection Service, the labor service units, and the Naval Historical Team.

The Baltic Fishery Protection Service was a cooperative project of The British Secret Intelligence Service (MI-6), the Royal Navy, the Gehlen Organization, and former German Navy personnel.[1] Fast German World War II boats called *Schnellboote* or *S-boote* (S-boats), manned by former German Kriegsmarine personnel and commanded by a former German S-boat officer, Hans-Helmut Klose, dropped off and picked up agents along the Baltic coast, carried out electronic surveillance of the coastline, and probed for coastal searchlights and radar. The S-boats operated for about seven years starting in 1949. They carried many agents in and retrieved about fifty.

In November 1950, only a few months after the outbreak of the Korean War, the U.S. Navy, acting through COMNAVGER, formed three labor service units in Germany "to assist in manning the ships, craft, and shore facilities of U.S. Naval Forces, Germany." The Naval Historical Team was asked to assist in identifying and recruiting appropriate personnel, especially former members of the World War II German Navy (Kriegsmarine). The three labor service units established were a small liaison group at COMNAVGER headquarters in Heidelberg, a mine-sweeping unit at the U.S. Navy base in Bremerhaven, and a small Rhine River Patrol with flotillas at Wiesbaden-Schierstein, Karlsruhe, and Mannheim. The labor service units were civilian in name only, for they were uniformed, housed, fed, and trained like U.S. Navy sailors. They were meant to be ready to enter the new German Navy when it was formed. The creation of the labor service

---

1. Douglas C. Peifer, *The Three German Navies* (Gainesville: University Press of Florida, 2002), 102–105.

units was an early step toward Germany's rearmament.

The Naval Historical Team, Bremerhaven, was a project of U.S. Naval Intelligence. The initial members wrote historical studies, but eventually the team's mission was changed to planning for and quietly organizing and coordinating efforts for the future German Navy. CAPT Arthur H. Graubart, then head of Naval Intelligence in Germany, stationed in Berlin, and his assistant LCDR Edwin Riedel first contacted German officers to ask for their cooperation in the project in 1948. The locus of support of the team was moved to the Munich naval intelligence office, and Rychly became the Navy's designated liaison to both the NHT admirals and the Gehlen Organization in nearby Pullach.

In its first months, the NHT produced many historical studies—of German Navy experience in Arctic operations, German harbor defenses, the effectiveness of Allied mines and German countermeasures, German knowledge of Allied Atlantic convoy routes. The NHT also studied some contemporary matters such as how to deny Soviet submarines access to the North Sea, how to close up the White Sea, and submarines and torpedo employment by the German Navy.

The Qualifications of the Four NHT Admirals

The credentials of the four NHT admirals who met with Val Rychly were impressive:

ADM Konrad Patzig was the oldest. He had served in the former German Navy and been chief of the Abwehr, Germany's military intelligence agency, for the short period 1933–35. Admiral Patzig clashed with some of Hitler's favorites, including Heinrich Himmler, head of the Nazi Reichssicherheitshauptamt (Reich Security Head Office, or RSHA) and of the dreaded Gestapo, and Reinhard Heydrich, head of the Nazi's Sicherheitsdienst (security police, or SD). Patzig resisted Himmler's attempt to take over the Abwehr and was consequently removed from his position as chief of the agency in 1935 and replaced by ADM Wilhelm Franz Canaris. Patzig became, for a while, chief of the naval personnel department. His resistance to Nazi Party control of the Navy brought him into disfavor with Hitler, and in consequence, he sat out World War II in positions of little influence.

Admiral Patzig was of special importance to the efforts to build a new German Navy because he had knowledge of most of the Kriegsmarine's higher officers and he knew who among them were Nazis and Nazi sympathizers. He sat on screening boards for denazification.

The Skipper admired Patzig for his courage and determination to stand by his principles. He showed me a photograph of Hitler at Kiel reviewing a group of Kriegsmarine officers and sailors. All were in dress uniforms, standing at attention; all, save one, held the right arm straight and high in the Nazi "Sieg Heil!" salute to the Führer. One officer in the front row held his right arm bent and his right hand at the beak of his Navy hat in the traditional military salute. It was, of course, Admiral Patzig.

ADM Friedrich Ruge was the most active and the most influential of the group. Like Patzig, he had many years experience in the former German Navy and rose to be the flag officer for the German fleet of minesweepers. He was the German Navy admiral at the Italian Naval High Command and finally was assigned in 1944 as the Navy's representative to Gen. Erwin Rommel's Army Group B in France. Ruge was charged with strengthening the coastal fortifications of France to resist the expected invasion attempt by the Western Allies.

The U.S. Navy paid particular attention to Admiral Ruge and considered him an able and reliable ally. In 1952 the Navy flew him to the United States for a lecture tour of the U.S. Naval War College in Newport, Rhode Island, and the Naval Academy in Annapolis, Maryland. The U.S. ambassador to West Germany discreetly indicated to Chancellor Adenauer that Ruge would be an excellent choice to head the future Bundesmarine. In 1955 Adenauer selected Admiral Ruge to head the naval section of the Ministry of Defense (the former Amt Blank) and chose Admiral Wagner to serve as his deputy. Admiral Ruge was the first chief of the new Bundesmarine, and Admiral Wagner was his successor. Thus two of the four members of Val Rychly's secret planning group were the first two commanders in chief of the new German Navy.

Ruge was fluent in English, acted as a translator at times, and authored historical research studies for both the U.S. Army and Navy. He had wide contacts with German Navy veterans. Like Patzig he was well connected, anti-Nazi, and politically acceptable to the Western Allies.

Admiral Ruge continued to visit the Skipper for years after they both were retired. Ruge was a scholarly and outgoing person. During my visit to the Skipper with my wife and children in 1975, we shared a summer afternoon with Admiral Ruge. After his retirement from the new German Navy, he had devoted himself to writing and teaching. He was appointed to a position at Tübingen University and was a visiting professor at the Citadel in South Carolina.

He was innovative. While serving as the German Navy representative to the Italian Navy during World War II, he found that the German junior officers assigned to assist him spoke no Italian and found it difficult to learn. He solved this problem by attaining the assignment of German officers who had studied Latin; they found it easy to learn Italian.

ADM Gerhard Wagner had joined the German Navy in 1916. For the last twelve years of his naval career he held offices in the Naval War Staff. He rose to higher and higher responsibilities, and from June 1941 until June 1944, he was the chief of the operations department of the Naval War Staff. From June 1944 until May 1945, he was admiral for special tasks attached to the supreme commander of the navy. In this capacity he served as a special assistant to ADM Karl Dönitz, whom Hitler named as his successor in the last days of the war. Admiral Wagner was called to testify in the Nuremburg War Crimes Tribunal's trial of Admiral Dönitz. A decade later, in the new German Navy, he was Admiral Ruge's deputy and followed Ruge as commander in chief.

ADM Helmuth Heye graduated from high school in Berlin in 1914 and joined the Kaiser's Imperial Navy, rising to command of the heavy cruiser *Admiral Hipper*. During the battle for Norway in April 1940, he encountered a British destroyer and sank it. *Admiral Hipper* stayed to rescue British survivors, and Heye sent a message to the British Admiralty through the Red Cross praising the gallantry of the British commander and crew. In subsequent assignments he commanded German naval forces in the Black Sea and became the admiral for the Midget Weapons Unit, a German Navy commando group similar to the U.S. Navy's underwater demolition teams. In the postwar period Heye published a number of works on naval matters. He joined Adenauer's party, the Christian Democratic Union (CDU), and was elected to the *Bundestag* of the new Federal Republic. He was appointed a member of its committee on military affairs.

North Korean Attack Spurs Western Rearmament
On June 25, 1950, North Korean forces, with the support of Stalin, attacked South Korea, and in the West concerns over Soviet intentions soared. If Stalin would risk starting a major war for so little potential gain as control of the rest of the Korean peninsula, what might he do to add Europe to the Soviet bloc? Interest in rearmament grew in West Germany as well as among the Western Allies. Admirals Patzig, Ruge, Wagner, and Heye were ready and able to lead rearmament

with respect to naval affairs. They were well connected to Chancellor Adenauer, the officials of the Amt Blank, and Gens. Adolf Heusinger and Hans Speidel, the military advisers to the Amt Blank.

17

THE GENERALS AND THE NEW ARMED FORCES: SOVEREIGNTY RESTORED AND NATO

Summer 1955

By the summer of 1955, after I had been in Munich about six months, I had learned much about the activities conducted at or from Possart Platz 3. With both O'Hearn and Aschenfelter gone, I took on their responsibilities as well as new ones from the Skipper. My principal intelligence duty was editing the intelligence reports translated into English by the German professional staff. Interrogating border crossers and others of possible interest to the Navy was an interesting but infrequent part of my duties. I was, in effect, the in-house manager of the German intelligence staff, except for the activities of Dr. Straimer.

In addition to editing reports and managing the German staff, I met regularly with the analysts who made up the Gehlen Organization's Navy EvaluationSection. I visited their offices in the compound at Pullach almost weekly and was always warmly received but not much happened during my visits. I obtained no new information about the Soviet bloc but was able to monitor the group's morale and occasionally help by delivering, from ONI, unclassified technical publications from the United States.

I knew that the Skipper had continuing contact with the top level of the Gehlen Organization, both with General Gehlen and with James Critchfield. I had served as a courier between the Skipper and Critchfield but I knew nothing of what I carried. And because I edited the reports of the Skipper's meetings with the German admirals, I was aware of their work toward the creation of the Bundesmarine.

My trip to Fürstenfeldbruck with the Skipper and Doktor Schneider (see chapter 1) was not the Skipper's only trip of this kind. Doktor Schneider was, of course, Gen. Reinhard Gehlen. The Navy airplane flew him and the Skipper to Naples, whence they went aboard a major aircraft carrier of the U.S. Sixth Fleet. I knew that the Skipper introduced top U.S. Navy officers to German officers and other officials to strengthen the already strong German ties to the United States. At various times the Skipper arranged for General Gehlen, General Heusinger, and a number of other German officers to spend several days aboard one of the Sixth Fleet's aircraft carriers so that they could observe carrier task force operations and the power and mobility of the U.S. Navy. The Skipper escorted his guests on these trips; I managed the office while he was away.

The Gehlen Organization and Former German Officers

In the summer of 1955 I was not aware of the large role played by the Gehlen Organization in assembling and providing employment and housing to hundreds of former officers of the German armed forces and especially former officers of the German Army's General Staff. I learned only later that former German generals Adolf Heusinger, Hans Speidel, and Friedrich Foertsch had played central roles in bringing about closer German ties with the United States, in rearming Germany, and in achieving German membership in the NATO alliance.

General Heusinger was chief of the Gehlen Organization's Evaluation Branch. He had been chief of the operations division of the German General Staff near the end of World War II. As such he had been General Gehlen's superior. In early 1945 Heusinger, like Gehlen, recognized the danger in the Russian advances and reported them accurately to Hitler. Hitler, however, would accept no bad news. Instead of facing the reality of the German Army's situation, Hitler removed Heusinger from his position.

During World War II Gen. Hans Speidel had been chief of staff to General Rommel during Rommel's tenure as commander of the forces assigned to resist the expected Allied invasion of continental Europe, Hitler's "Fortress Europa." Speidel had volunteered and served in World War I, then entered the postwar Reichswehr (army) as an officer and simultaneously studied at various German universities. He received his doctorate in 1925. From 1930 to 1933 he was in training at the General Staff School. Following his training he held a number of assignments on the Western Front, including command of troops in the invasion of France.

Heusinger and Speidel were longtime friends and comrades in arms. They took their three-year General Staff training at the same time and intermittently crossed paths thereafter. Neither was a Nazi Party member or sympathizer. The Gestapo arrested both after the July 20, 1944, attempt on Hitler's life by Count Claus von Stauffenberg. Both were suspected of complicity in the assassination plot, but both were cleared and returned to duty.

Near the end of World War II both Heusinger and Speidel reached the same conclusions that Gehlen had reached: that the war was lost, that there would be a new democratic Germany someday, that it would need armed forces, and that it should ally itself with the West, as led by the United States, to protect itself against the Soviet Union's military power.

A third officer from the General Staff, Gen. Friedrich Foertsch, held the same opinions as Heusinger and Speidel and formed part of a triumvirate within the Gehlen Organization planning for the rearmament of a sovereign Germany allied with the West. This triumvirate, working in secrecy, had the silent support of General Gehlen and many other former officers. Working in cooperation with the German admirals, the three became the principal architects of the new German armed forces and of NATO's commitment to a line of defense along the Elbe River, i.e., a defense of West Germany.

In 1948 Gehlen was rapidly expanding his organization and persuaded Heusinger to accept appointment as overall chief of the Evaluation Branch. This provided Heusinger a modest income, a house, access to intelligence, a cover for his planning activities, and contact with the Americans. James Critchfield, the CIA chief at the Pullach compound, relates that he held many conversations with Heusinger, sometimes over dinner at Heusinger's house, and became his friend. Speidel lived outside the Pullach compound but had strong ties to Heusinger and Foertsch.

We know that Val Rychly's secret guided tours to the Sixth Fleet were effective in bolstering the German officers' pro-American leanings. Critchfield writes in *Partners at the Creation*,

> One day Heusinger disappeared from Pullach for almost a week. When he returned he gave me a glowing account of his experience as a guest of the captain of one of the large carriers participating in a U.S. Sixth Fleet training maneuver in the Mediterranean. Heusinger was deeply impressed by the appearance and performance of the pilots and crews of the carrier. He added that Commander Rychly had arranged and escorted him on his visit to the Sixth Fleet, for which he was deeply

appreciative. For a future top officer in the Bundeswehr, this had been an important experience.[1]

A Defense Policy and Rearmament in West Germany

Kim Il Sung, the communist dictator of Stalin's client state, North Korea, can be credited with spurring rapid rearmament in the West. The June 25, 1950, North Korean attack on South Korea sent a shock wave through the West, for it showed Stalin to be willing to risk war in order to gain his goals.

Chancellor Adenauer recognized that West Germany had only partial sovereignty: it had no defense ministry, no armed forces, and no defense plans. He knew that he needed to do more to protect Germany's interests and to have influence in the future of Europe. In July 1950 the chancellor secretly asked his aides to obtain a broad think piece, an evaluation of Germany's strategic situation and recommendations for Germany's response. To prepare this think piece, Chancellor Adenauer's staff turned to the triumvirate of generals—Heusinger, Speidel, and Foertsch—who had been studying and planning armed forces to meet Germany's future needs. Adenauer received their report in early August 1950 and was deeply impressed by the *Sommer Denkschrift* (Summer Think Piece).

Major themes of the generals' report were that Europe was so divided that it could not defend itself unless joined and led by the United States, so Germany should work for such an alliance, rearm, and contribute armed forces to the alliance. Adenauer agreed and planned to make the Sommer Denkschrift the foundation of his defense policy and his foreign policy.

In early October 1950, to broaden support for the policies of the Sommer Denkschrift, Adenauer, in complete secrecy, assembled a small conference at the Hillerod Abbey near Bonn. The conference, charged to recommend to him a defense policy, was dominated by the pro-American generals and admirals with whom the Skipper had been working. Of the fifteen participants, five were former German Army officers, including Generals Heusinger, Speidel, and Foertsch and COL Eberhard Graf von Nostiz (another Gehlen Organization member). In addition, at least three participants were former German Navy

---

1. James H. Critchfield, *Partners at the Creation: The Men behind Postwar Germany's Defense and Intelligence Establishments* (Annapolis, MD: Naval Institute Press, 2003), 103.

officers, including VADM Friedrich Ruge and CAPT Alfred Schulze-Hinrichs, a member of the Gehlen Organization's Navy Evaluation Section. The basic agenda for discussion was the Sommer Denkschrift. The participants broke into four work groups, three chaired by Heusinger, Speidel, and Foerstch, respectively, and one by a former German Air Force general. Not surprisingly, the conference endorsed the provisions of the Sommer Denkschrift and provided further details. The conference report was unanimous, signed by all the participants. The chancellor adopted the unanimous recommendations of the conference as his defense policy.

Implementation of the Defense Policy

The chancellor moved quickly to organize for the defense policy's implementation. By the end of October 1950 he created a shadow ministry of defense headed by Theodor Blank that came to be known as the *Amt Blank* (Blank Office). Heusinger and Speidel became the chancellor's chief military advisers. Admiral Ruge was his chief adviser on naval matters.

By the end of 1950 the chancellor had a defense policy and advisers, but the Western Allies had not yet reached a consensus as to Germany's future role in the Western Alliance. The Soviet Union continued its efforts to prevent West Germany from rearming or allying itself with the Western powers. From 1951 to 1955, negotiations among the Western powers and the Federal Republic were almost continuous but progress toward agreement was slow. Heusinger and Speidel represented the Federal Republic in these negotiations. The positions of the parties were:

- France opposed any German rearmament and had no enthusiasm for reunification of West and East Germany.
- Britain had deep concern about German rearmament but was more amenable to compromise and to acceptance of U.S. leadership.
- The United States wanted a well-organized and binding international alliance, including the Federal Republic, under American leadership. The Federal Republic was to rearm, join the alliance, and contribute to its armed forces.
- The Federal Republic agreed with the U.S. position, provided the alliance would treat it as an equal and would defend West Germany (i.e., at the Elbe River), not sacrifice Germany and fall back to the Rhine or any other more westerly line of defense.

The negotiators finally agreed to form a European defense community, with Germany included. The French parliament refused to approve this proposal, however, and negotiations had to be resumed.

The Soviets made a last-ditch attempt to prevent Germany from joining the Western powers. In January and February 1954 a four-power conference on German reunification was held in Berlin, but it accomplished nothing, and it reinforced the Western powers' determination to reach agreement without the Soviet Union and without reunification at that time.

Paris Agreements, 1954–55: Restoration of Full Sovereignty, Rearmament, and NATO

New agreements were reached among the Western powers and the Federal Republic, and on October 23, 1954, papers were signed in Paris. The Federal Republic was invited to join NATO and permitted to rearm and contribute armed forces to the alliance. The Federal Republic would enter the alliance as an equal, and NATO would defend West Germany at the Elbe. The Federal Republic was also invited to join the Western European Union. Full sovereignty for the Federal Republic was to come into effect on May 5, 1955. Implementation of the Paris Agreements stretched into 1956 and beyond.

The Soviet Union responded quickly to the agreement by creating a military alliance with its Eastern European satellites, including East Germany, called the Warsaw Pact. Prospects for reunification did not look good.

As the Federal Republic achieved full sovereignty the Amt Blank evolved into the West German Defense Ministry, with General Heusinger as chief of the military division, General Speidel chief of the division handling international affairs such as dealings with NATO, and Admiral Ruge heading the Navy division. Later all three held prominent positions in the NATO command. Heusinger was chosen by Adenauer as the first chief of staff of the Bundeswehr (West German armed forces) while Speidel rose to commander (*Oberbefehlshaber*) of the Allied Land Forces in Middle Europe. New German armed forces were established: the army organized in armored and mobile divisions, and the navy and air force organized appropriately for their missions.

Rychly's Friends and Colleagues Move to Positions of Authority

In 1955 and 1956, as planned, most of Val Rychly's German staff, friends, and colleagues moved into positions of authority in the new armed forces or civilian agencies of the Federal Republic. Admiral Ruge became the first chief of the new German Navy and was followed in this position by Admiral Wagner. Both had been members of the planning group that met in the Skipper's house in Munich.

Karl Hetz of Possart Platz 3 returned to duty in the new navy. I was told later that he served for some time as head of German Naval Intelligence and won promotion to the rank of admiral. Helmuth Pich of Possart Platz 3 went into the new navy and became its director of communications. Dr. Straimer of Possart Platz 3 was appointed to a high position in the Federal Republic's scientific work. I was once told that he joined the Atom Ministerium (Ministry of Atomic Affairs). Max Parnitzki stayed at Possart Platz 3 for six years, taking on more and more responsibilities, but in April 1962 he accepted a position in the Press and Information Office of the Federal Chancellor's Office. Max supervised a large group of analysts and journalists who monitored publications and broadcasts from the communist world and prepared daily summary briefings for the chancellor and top executive branch and parliamentary leaders. Albrecht "Sepp" Obermaier of the Gehlen Organization's Navy Evaluation Section, a former S-boat commander, joined the new navy and became commander of NATO's Baltic Sea Forces. The leadership positions achieved by the staff members of Possart Platz 3 and the Gehlen Organization in the new German government owe much to the years of quiet, secret work of CDR Val Rychly.

18

ADENAUER VISITS MOSCOW, SEPTEMBER 9–13, 1955

The struggle between the Western Allies and the Soviet Union over the future of Germany came to decision in the Paris Agreements of 1954. The full sovereignty provision took effect on May 5, 1955.

There remained many issues to settle in order to define the future relations between West Germany and the Soviet Union. Ten years had passed since the end of the war, but there were still bitter animosities between the Germans and the Russians. Neither could ignore the other, however. When Soviet Premier Nikolay Bulganin and First Secretary of the Communist Party Nikita Khrushchev invited Adenauer to visit Moscow in the fall of 1955, Adenauer felt bound to accept the invitation. For the Soviets the biggest issue was trade; for Adenauer it was the return of thousands of German prisoners of war and civilians still held by the Soviets ten years after the end of the war.

The precise numbers were, and are still, difficult to determine, but the West German government charged that over a million German soldiers had been reported as missing in action on the East Front, of whom 10 percent, it believed, were still alive. In addition, the German government stated that two hundred thousand Germans were working as slave labor in the uranium mines of the East Zone and fifty thousand more were in other forced labor camps. Illustrating the scale of the Germans' concerns, West Germany charged that from Lower Saxony alone seven hundred fifty thousand Germans were transported to Soviet camps in the last months of the war.[1] There had been repatriations in the decade since the end of the war, of course, but not enough to account for the numbers missing. The fate of missing

---

1. Eugene Davidson, *The Death and Life of Germany: An Account of the American Occupation* (New York: Knopf, 1959), 357–358; Keesing's

German soldiers and civilians remained a source of grief and anxiety throughout Germany.

Bulganin's reply was brief: the Soviet Union held fewer than ten thousand German prisoners of war and they were war criminals.

Adenauer's visit was set to begin on September 9, 1955, in Moscow. Both sides prepared carefully for these crucially important talks. The feelings, tone and outcome of the talks were described by Smyser in his book, *From Yalta to Berlin*:

> Adenauer did not relish going to Moscow. . . . He knew that the Soviets wanted to talk mainly about trade, but he wanted to talk about prisoners. . . . Adenauer and the Soviet leaders had no friendly chit-chat. In bitterly disputatious talks, Khrushchev besmirched the Germans as followers of Nazism. Adenauer replied that it was Molotov who had signed the treaty with Hitler that had led to World War II through the 1939 invasion of Poland. Adenauer denounced the behavior of Soviet soldiers in Germany. Khrushchev replied in kind about German soldiers in the Soviet Union. Whenever Khrushchev talked about trade, Adenauer talked about prisoners of war. At one point, with the negotiations completely stalled, Adenauer instructed his pilot to file a return flight plan. This broke the deadlock, but Adenauer and Khrushchev needed several more days to establish diplomatic relations.[2]

All topics of discussion proved contentious. The parties agreed to recognize each other and exchange ambassadors. Adenauer achieved his purpose of bringing out at least some prisoners of war, but the numbers were disappointing. Out of over a million German soldiers that were unaccounted for, Moscow would release only 9,626 as well as about twenty thousand civilians.[3] Khrushchev in turn achieved his purpose of increasing trade. They had done what they had to do, but each had swallowed a bitter pill.

The Soviet Plan to Assassinate Adenauer

The days leading up to the Moscow meeting had been a time of extra

---

Research Report, *Germany and Eastern Europe since 1945: From the Potsdam Agreement to Chancellor Brandt's "Ostpolitik"* (New York: Charles Scribner's Sons, 1973).

2. W. R. Smyser, *From Yalta to Berlin: The Cold War Struggle over Germany* (New York: St. Martin's Griffin, 1999), 132.

3. Smyser, *From Yalta to Berlin*, 132.

tension. West Germany's new sovereignty and alliance with the West had angered the Soviets. Chancellor Adenauer championed the pro-West policy and was a serious obstacle to all Soviet hopes of hegemony in Germany. Adenauer was an elderly man—almost eighty years old—and somewhat frail, but his will and persistence were remarkable.

I became involved in this story in a most unexpected way in late August or early September 1955. One late summer day the Skipper was out of the office, so I was in charge. That afternoon I heard Dr. Straimer ask Joe if Commander Rychly was present. "No, but Lieutenant Durning is here," came Joe's reply. There was a pause; I could almost hear Dr. Straimer's thoughts as he considered whether he could speak with me. "Good. Please tell him I would like to speak with him—alone, and at once, if possible." I came out of my office and greeted him. Noting the urgency in his voice and his desire to speak with me alone, I led him into the Skipper's office and closed the heavy door behind us.

Dr. Straimer started our conversation in German and spoke very quickly. I repeated in English any part of which I was not certain.

"I have just returned from Bonn where I attended a small meeting of the Chancellor's aides concerning security arrangements for his trip to Moscow," said Dr. Straimer. "I was invited to the discussion because of my background in physics and radiation. What I heard was surprising . . . and I think that it will be of interest in Washington."

"Please go on," I replied. Straimer reported that the Germans had sent a team of technical experts to Moscow to survey the security measures to be taken to protect the chancellor and his aides. They performed electronic sweeps and other investigations of the quarters in which the Russians intended to house the chancellor and his party during the visit. The search found a great number of concealed listening devices throughout the quarters, and to its surprise, the security team found in the wall of the bedroom to be used by the chancellor a concealed source of high-intensity radiation (probably cobalt) positioned and designed so as to irradiate Adenauer as he slept. In short, the Soviets had planned to kill the elderly chancellor by radiation whose effects would show up only after his return to Germany and be attributed to other causes.

The plan to kill Adenauer raised questions about the Soviets' next steps. What were their intentions? Did they plan other actions against the political leadership of the Federal Republic? Did they plan to destabilize the Federal Republic, cause chaos, and intervene with the huge Soviet Army to "restore order"?

In the aftermath of the security team's report, the German government had to consider its options. Would it postpone or even cancel the negotiations or simply insist on different quarters and time to investigate them? The Soviets had clearly planned secret harm to the chancellor, but they would not dare to do that harm in any way attributable to them.

Dr. Straimer and I agreed that this information should go to Washington as quickly as possible. I assured him I would try to find Val Rychly immediately. I would start work at once on a written report of what he had told me and would go over my draft with him to be sure it was correct. Dr. Straimer went to his office. I called in Joe and told him that we would work on a report starting immediately and continue for as long as it took. The report would be Top Secret. Only the Skipper, Dr. Straimer, Joe, and I were to know of this. The office workday was almost over, so the other yeomen could leave in a few minutes, but we would remain.

I called the Skipper's house from the telephone on my desk. Fortunately, Frau Mattheus knew the Skipper's whereabouts and how to reach him. She contacted him and asked him to phone me. In just a few minutes he called, and we had a veiled conversation in which I told him that someone he knew very well had brought some urgent and important news, about which I sought his instructions, but that I doubted that I should speak of it on my telephone line. He agreed but said he would call me back in about thirty minutes from a more secure phone and would call to a special secure phone in his office.

His call came on time. I read him my draft report. He approved it and agreed that I should give it a high priority, classify it Top Secret, and carry out all the requirements set out in the Navy Security Manual. I should address and send the message to the director of Naval Intelligence and no one else. I should encrypt the text using a one-time pad several of which I would find in a certain drawer in the giant safe in his office. He gave me the combination with instructions about the combination's use. I could sign the report myself "by direction" from him. The one-time pad included instructions for its use and disposal after use.

I worked in his office with the door locked for an hour or two and then gave the encrypted message to Joe to type. I then put all papers about the report, along with the one-time pad, in the drawer in the safe where I found the pad and locked the safe. I then had Joe drive me with the encrypted message to the American consulate, identified myself to the guards and the communications watch officer, and asked the officer to send the encrypted message with a high priority. The consulate's communications staff were familiar with the existence of our office and often handled communications for us.

It was late when Joe and I returned to Possart Platz 3, but I sat down and read the relevant portions of the security manual again to be sure we had done everything required and then closed the offices. Val would be back in the office the next day. He offered no information as to where he was, and I did not ask.

To my surprise, when I arrived at the office the next morning I had a message from the communications watch officer at the consulate asking me to call. I did so at once and was told that the consulate had a message for me in a code its staff could not decipher. The watch officer was rather unhappy about this, saying they had wasted a lot of time trying. He curtly asked me to come and get my message at once since it had a high priority designation. Joe took me again to the consulate, where I signed for the message and collected it. I offered no explanation about the cipher for the consulate had no need to know.

We drove quickly back to Possart Platz 3, where I again locked myself in the Skipper's office and, using the one-time pad instructions, deciphered the brief message, which was from the director of Naval Intelligence. The director ranked our report as top priority and ordered us to stay in close contact with our source and report immediately any additional information received. He also ordered us to send by separate top secret message, using another one-time pad, full information about our source, so ONI could evaluate his or her reliability.

I began drafting a report about Dr. Straimer, but fearful of making a mistake, I waited for the Skipper to return to finish it. He returned in the early afternoon, and we worked on a brief biography of Dr. Straimer, pointing out his qualifications as a physicist familiar with radiation and his close association with high-ranking political leaders, especially Franz Joseph Strauss, leader of the Christian Social Union (CSU), the large Bavarian party that partnered with Adenauer's Christian Democratic Union (CDU) to help make a majority in the Bundestag. We stressed also his work with the International Red Cross and the many valuable reports he had written over the years, all of which had proved reliable. We did not reveal his name, instead sending it to the DNI separately by Navy courier mail, cross-referenced to our biographical report.

Chancellor Adenauer kept his appointment with Bulganin and Khrushchev for negotiations in Moscow. Different quarters—safer and more secure—were found. Chancellor Adenauer visited Moscow September 9–13, 1955. He was a courageous man.

19

THE RETURN OF GERMAN
PRISONERS OF WAR

German-Soviet POW Agreement: Bulganin's Promise

Ten years had passed since the German surrender in May 1945 ended the fighting in Europe in World War II. The war's death toll, the servicemen missing in action, and the disappearance of soldiers into prisoner of war camps were in 1955 still unhealed wounds that changed the lives of tens of millions of people who had lost spouses, parents, siblings, and children. Human losses and injuries were heavy in all the theaters of the war, but nowhere were they greater than on the East Front, the site of the colossal struggle between the German and the Soviet armies from Leningrad to the Caucasus and in all the lands between Berlin and Moscow.

The number of casualties suffered in World War II is uncertain, but conservatively stated, several million German servicemen were known to have died in combat, most of them on the East Front. To this loss must be added the hundreds of thousands—perhaps a million or more—missing in action and the hundreds of thousands taken by the Soviets as prisoners of war. Almost every German home had reason to grieve the death, disappearance, or imprisonment of a father, husband, brother, or son sent to battle in the East. For many of these homes there remained an especially painful wound as they did not know what had happened to their loved ones. Had they died in battle? Had they been captured and imprisoned?

The fate of German prisoners of war still held captive in the Soviet Union was a very important political issue in the Federal Republic. The West German government estimated the number of these not-yet-returned prisoners of war to be hundreds of thousands, but the Soviets did not agree to this estimate. Many thousands of POWs had been returned to West Germany and East Germany by 1955 and many more had died. Soviet authorities insisted that in the summer of 1955 they held only about 10,000 German prisoners of war, all of whom, they said, were war criminals. The German-Soviet negotiations were successful in part. The parties agreed to exchange ambassadors, and as for the POWs, Premier Bulganin insisted only 9,626 remained in the Soviet Union. He promised to return them.

Pursuant to Bulganin's promise, the repatriation of the remaining German POWs began the very next month, October 1955. Arrangements had been made to deliver the repatriates (*Wiederheimkehrer*) by train to Friedland, a station on the West German border. At Friedland the trains would stop, and the repatriates would disembark the train and walk across a neutral space and through a gate into West Germany. A group of West German border guards, other officials, journalists, and ordinary people hopeful of finding a missing loved one stood just beyond the gate. As each repatriate stepped through the gate, a German official asked him to state his name, military rank, unit, the place where he was captured, and home address. Everything said was broadcast by radio throughout the country.

Tension was high throughout Germany. The Soviets gave no advance notice or schedule of POW trains—but on October 6, 1955, the first train arrived at Friedland.

Voices from the Past

Near my former apartment in the Schumann Strasse was a neighborhood restaurant that served good *bürgerliches Essen* (plain food) at moderate prices. I became a frequent guest and struck up a friendly rapport with the waitress, who wore a black dress and clean white apron. It was a comfortable place, and I could practice my German through conversation with the waitress about food, beer, and the weather or bring along a German newspaper and struggle to read the long sentences with verbs trailing at the end. Almost every day the lead story was about the war in Korea or rather, the post-armistice negotiations at the round table in Panmunjon. I still remember some of the long words and phrases with which an article typically began: "*Die angehende Waffenstillstandverhandlungen bei Panmunjon führt gestern weiter—aber ohne Fortschritt . . .*" (The on-going armistice negotiations at Panmunjon continued yesterday—but without progress . . .)

The restaurant was small, about ten tables, and filled up each evening with neighborhood residents—singles, couples, and families. German reserve approaches that of the British, so I never got beyond *Guten Abend* (Good evening) with any of the guests at the other tables. It is well that I didn't try, for the restaurant's radio was tuned to *Bayerische Rundfunk* (Bavarian Radio) and lovely classical music—by Haydn, Mozart, Beethoven, and other classical composers—played softly in the background. And, in addition, when I was not reading a newspaper, I enjoyed watching the ordinary life of the Bavarian middle class and absorbing the room's comfortable ambiance. German has an untranslatable word for that special comfortable, friendly ambiance: the restaurant was *gemütlich*.

On the evening of October 6, 1955, I was having dinner at the restaurant. The tables were full. There was laughter and sounds of children being scolded and taught restaurant behavior. Suddenly the music stopped and a deep and somber voice said (as translated into English): "Bavarian Radio interrupts this broadcast to bring you important news—the first train of repatriated German prisoners of war (Wiederheimkehrer) has arrived at Friedland."

Immediately all conversation in the restaurant stopped. All eating stopped. Knives, forks, and spoons were put on plates. The restaurant was still; the tension almost palpable. Then, from the radio: "The repatriates have left the train, they are gathering in lines . . . and now the first is stepping through the gate to the Federal Republic—and to freedom."

And then the voice of the returning soldier (names and identifications not real), answering questions from the reception group: "Erich Strohmayer. Sergeant, Third Panzer Division, captured July 15, 1943, at the Battle of Kursk, USSR, home city, Ulm."

Silence. Then radio: "Hans Schumacher. Twelfth Armored Infantry, captured January 1943 at Stalingrad, home, Stuttgart. Peter Backmeier, Nineteenth Artillery, captured near Leningrad, 1944, home, Mannheim."

And so it went, on and on, sometimes for hours. Trains arrived at irregular intervals, without prior notice, and at all hours. When a train arrived all Germany stopped to listen; the whole nation held its breath. Newspapers reported and showed photos of joyful reunions of husbands and wives, parents and sons.

But on October 20 the trains stopped coming. By then only 5,863 out of the promised 9,626 POWs had arrived. The Soviets offered no explanation. The West German press speculated that problems had arisen in the negotiations about the details of the exchange of embassies, and Soviet demands for forced repatriation of Soviet citizens living in Germany regardless of the person's own wishes to stay in Germany.

On December 11, without prior notice or explanation, trains began arriving again and continued until the promised number of prisoners—9,626—had been delivered. The rest of the hundreds of thousands of POWs sought by the West German government have never been accounted for. Probably, they died in Soviet captivity.

Frau Raab kept a radio in the kitchen at Possart Platz 3; like thousands of other German women, she listened, hoped, and cried. Her husband was listed as missing on the East Front. He was not on any of the trains. Her last hope was gone. She put on her white dress and served us mid-morning coffee, as she did every day.

PART 4

ENDURING FRIENDSHIPS

20

HELMUTH AND MAX: LATER YEARS

Germany's transformation from enemy to ally in a little over one decade required that millions of Americans, Britons, French, and others soften their just anger against the Germans and that millions of Germans come out of denial and create a democratic state. On the large scale of nation-states this was accomplished, and on the scale of individuals change sometimes went further, allowing enduring friendships. So it was with Helmuth Pich, Max Parnitzki, and me.

Helmuth Pich

When the new German Navy was founded, Helmuth applied and was accepted as the director of naval communications.

He married, and when he retired, he and his wife, Hildegard, settled in a modernized former farmhouse in Geesthacht, a suburb of Hamburg. I visited Helmuth and Hildegard several times in Geesthacht, and once they came to see me and my family at the Parnitzkis' house in Bonn. Helmuth tried to visit me when he was in Washington, D.C., with a NATO group. Unfortunately we did not connect that time.

During my last visit with Helmuth in Geesthacht, in May 1996, he told me that the British pilot of the plane that attacked his submarine in the Indian Ocean had traced him through British and German navy records and called on him at Geesthacht. The British pilot was a talented painter and gave Helmuth a painting depicting the event in the Indian Ocean. The painting was displayed in a prominent place on Helmuth and Hildegard's living room wall. It was an important sign of the mutual respect between the two former enemies and, more broadly, a sign of the healing of relations between British and German warriors of World War ll.

A formal black-bordered printed card bearing sad news of Helmuth's death arrived at our house in the spring of 1997. It read,

Helmuth Pich

Fregattenkapitän a.D.

26. Juni 1914 18. März 1997

Babziens/Ostpr. Geesthacht

Hildegard enclosed a kind note and some photos taken in 1996, during our last visit with the Pichs.

Max Parnitzki

I was close with Helmuth, but I became even closer with Max. Maximilian Parnitzki was a twentieth-century German-Russian Everyman. He was a full participant in the turmoil and violence of World War II and its aftermath. He knew the disappointment of a university education lost, the pride of military victory, the despair of military defeat, the hopelessness of a years-long imprisonment in Russia as a POW, and the personal victory of self-education and success in important service to his country—and to the free world.

Max and Waldtraut, his wife, met while both were employed at Possart Platz 3 and saw each other frequently outside the office. Although their courtship was in full force while I was in Munich, and although Max brought Waldtraut on some of our *Ausflüge*, they were so discreet that I never suspected the seriousness of their ties. They were married in Hamburg, Waldtraut's home, in March 1956. They had two daughters, Marion and Petra, both of whom completed university degrees and have risen to responsible positions in their chosen careers. With parents as intelligent and diligent as Max and Waldtraut, they could not fail.

Fortune smiled on me when it sent me to Munich to serve at Possart Platz 3. This allowed me to meet Max and start a lasting friendship that included our wives and children. My family and I visited the Parnitzki family in Germany a number of times after my year there with the Navy, and the Parnitzkis visited us in America. Their daughter Petra lived with us for a year while we were in Washington, D.C., and I was working for the Carter administration, and our daughter Susan stayed with them during part of her term of college study in Germany. Max and Waldtraut, their daughters, and sons-in-law, and grandchildren are our "European family," and we are their "American family."

Max and I had long conversations about history, anthropology, politics, family and children, the psychology of individuals and nations in war and in peace, and the history of languages. Sometimes, after we both had married, we were joined in our discussions by my wife Jean, Waldtraut, and their daughters. Discussions often began at breakfast and lasted for hours, through cup after cup of coffee.

Years with the U.S. Navy, 1952-62

Max stayed at Possart Platz 3 for ten years, until April 1962. He rose from a position as only a translator to responsibilities as an interrogator, intelligence analyst and evaluator, and expert about the Soviet Union and the Communist bloc. Val Rychly's replacement, CDR Chester J. Oleniacz, U.S. Navy, wrote of Max on his departure from Possart Platz 3 on April 12, 1962,

> His duties, as supervisory military intelligence research analyst consisted of the preparation of studies of maritime and naval matters. In addition he supervised the research and translation activities of several employees, competently and efficiently.
>
>   Mr. Parnitzki displayed the highest qualities of leadership and demonstrated exceptional knowledge of his assignments carrying them out with maximum effectiveness. His astuteness, keen judgment, knowledgeability and capacity for original and professional work is most favorably reflected in his outstanding performance.

A copy of this letter is appendix C. Its high praise and personal warmth are typical of the opinions and feelings of others who worked with Max.

Bundes Presse- und Informationsamt, 1962-80

In 1962 Max accepted appointment to an important position in the Federal Press and Information Office (Bundes Presse- und Informationsamt), part of the Office of the Chancellor (Bundeskanzleramt), and the Parnitzkis moved to Bonn. Max was responsible for producing a daily short summary of news and information for the chancellor, the leaders of the principal ministries, and the leaders of the Bundestag (parliament). The summary covered the most important announcements and reports from the media of the Communist-ruled lands (from Moscow and Prague to Beijing and Hanoi).

Max was responsible for preparing and publishing a longer daily report covering a selection of the most important reports, speeches, clarifications, articles, and comments released by the Communist press agencies and in Communist radio broadcasts. It was a stressful job. He supervised a staff of experts covering various countries and subjects as well as technical persons who monitored and taped radio broadcasts. The volume of material flowing in was immense. Once Max took me with him to his office on a Sunday afternoon. We stopped to talk with a technician operating a large room of giant recording machines all taping monitored broadcasts. At the time I was there, the technician was recording a speech of one of the leaders of Communist China at a Communist Party conference. He had already been speaking for four or five hours when we arrived!

Max retired from the Press and Information Office in 1980 and did some work as a freelance journalist, writing on matters concerning the Soviet bloc.

Everyman

In all my visits with Max I never heard him speak ill of anyone or complain about the hardships he had endured. Max was a positive thinker, alert to problems but quick to see opportunities in them. He was strongly opposed to communism, but not to Russians. He was intensely critical of Hitler, the Nazi Party, and the Holocaust, and conscious of the evils done by Germany under Hitler. But he was still a German citizen loyal to his comrades in arms and optimistic about the future of the German people when organized as a democracy and linked to the West.

Max was highly intelligent, with a genius for languages. He was also loyal, responsible, generous, and a warm-hearted friend. He was an admirable and effective human with a big heart, all in all *ein guter Kerl* (a good fellow). Max lived the life of the twentieth-century European, both its heights and its depths. Max was Everyman, and Max was my friend.

Max suffered a heart attack while playing tennis and died on January 18, 1982.

21

VLADIMIR RYCHLY

CDR Vladimir Rychly, U.S. Navy Reserve, "the Skipper," wasn't your typical American naval officer. He wasn't your typical officer or your typical American. He was unique—one of a kind—an unshakably patriotic American from Chicago; the son of immigrant Czech parents; an outstanding, perhaps even child-prodigy, violinist trained for ten years at a conservatory in Prague; and a naturally talented linguist who spoke English, German, and Czech fluently and had good command of Russian and other Slavic languages. Most important, he was a genius at understanding people, at gathering important intelligence, and at influencing, through sincere friendships, the decisions of persons of authority, including key decisions determining the course of German, and hence European, history in the Cold War years.

I kept in touch with Val Rychly in the decades following my service in Munich and visited him on a number of occasions in his home in the suburbs of Munich. We had long talks over meals that continued in the comfortable living room of the house, in the large rose garden behind the house, or on walks in the nearby Grünwald Forest. Val and I became ever-closer friends as the years went by, and he told me more about the intelligence activities in which I had participated, observed, or guessed at during my time at Possart Platz 3.

Several books have been published about Germany's transition from a defeated enemy to a valued ally of the Western powers and about the creation of democratic Germany's new armed forces. None has told the story of Val Rychly's important contribution to this transition or given credit to the U.S. Navy and its Office of Naval Intelligence for their farseeing support of Val's efforts. His activities at the time were carried out almost entirely outside of public view, most of it classified "Secret" or "Top Secret" because of its importance to U.S. national security.

Early Life in Chicago and Prague

Val Rychly was born in Chicago in 1909. He had a lonely, grim, almost Dickensian, childhood. His parents were immigrants to the United States from Czechoslovakia. His father was a baker; his mother was ill throughout his childhood and was confined to a hospital. Even as a young child Val was unusually talented at playing the violin, and his father dreamed that his son would become a concert violinist. In furtherance of his dream, his father took Val, when he was only seven years old, to Prague and enrolled him in a conservatory of music, leaving Val to live and board at the conservatory, while he himself returned to Chicago.

Val spent a long and lonely ten years at the conservatory. He lived in a tiny room and was almost always hungry. He learned music and a number of languages. He made good progress on the violin, but when he was seventeen, he injured his left hand, reportedly from too much practicing. The injury made it impossible for him to continue on the violin, so Val went back to Chicago, fluent in English, Czech, and probably German and Russian. He may also have learned other Slavic languages while he was in Prague.

Back in Chicago, Val's father told his son that he could no longer support him. Val, seventeen years old, was on his own. He worked at a variety of jobs to support himself and to continue his education in night classes at Northwestern University. He worked at an export-import firm, taught at a Czech school, worked at the Chicago World's Fair, and also gave the morning news in Czech at a Czech-language radio station in Chicago.

Entering the Navy

December 7, 1941, brought dramatic change. The Japanese attack on Pearl Harbor and Germany's declaration of war against the United States shortly thereafter sent the country into rapid mobilization. Val, like millions of other young Americans, suddenly faced military service. He finished college and received a notice from his draft board that he would be called up. He volunteered to enter the Navy. Val's wife, Hannelore, once told me that the Navy recruiters asked Val, "What can you do?" to which he replied, "Nothing, but I speak eleven languages."

The recruiters thought the Navy could use Val's linguistic talents and he was accepted.

Naval Intelligence Service, 1942-62: An Overview

Val served on active duty in naval intelligence for the next twenty years, from 1942 to 1962. His assignments during this period were remarkable: he interrogated POWs from the German Navy, especially U-boat officers; he worked with British secret intelligence (MI-6) in a race with the Russians to find and hold German scientists and other persons of interest at the war's end; he was a U.S. naval attaché accredited to Prague, Belgrade, and Warsaw; he was a U.S. observer in the United Nations' Palestine mission led by Count Bernadotte of Sweden; and then, for twelve years, he was founder and commanding officer of the Navy's intelligence office in Munich, Germany.

Val never talked much about his duties with MI-6 or as a member of the UN mission—that is, about his life from the end of the war in Europe on May 8, 1945, to his arrival to open the office in Munich in late 1948—but I have a copy of a travel diary kept in Val's own handwriting, the diary of "Vladimir L. Rychly, LT. USNR 401496," which sheds light on his whereabouts during this period. The diary is a day-by-day record of his travels, the people he met, and the meals and entertainments he enjoyed over a period of about three and a half years, from May 25, 1945 (two weeks after the German surrender), until January 23, 1949, in the midst of the Berlin blockade. Folded into the diary was U.S. Diplomatic Passport No. 1289 issued April 15, 1946, to Vladimir L. Rychly. It describes Val Rychly as a naval attaché accredited at the U.S. embassies at Belgrade, Yugoslavia; Warsaw, Poland; and Prague, Czechoslovakia. Copies of some sample pages from the diary make up Appendix E.

Naval Service in World War II, 1942-45: Interrogator of German POWs

At first, Val was assigned to interrogate captured enemy seamen or deserters—from Germany, Italy, or the Balkan states. I especially recall his telling me of his experience interrogating captured German U-boat officers at a POW detention facility near Washington, D.C. He was proud of his unit's successes in obtaining information and proud of the variety and ingenuity of their interrogation techniques. He told with amusement of his "tough duty" escorting some cooperative German officers on a one-day parole visit to Washington, D.C. It was a hot and humid day—too hot for sightseeing, so they found an air-conditioned bar, where they consumed vast quantities of cold beer.

He stressed that small courtesies and respect shown to the captive officers brought additional cooperation and useful information. It was typical of his method—warm to each person, sensitive to their interests, friendly, and reliable.

From the End of War in Europe to the Arrival in Munich, May 1945 to late 1948

Val told me something of his activities from the end of the war in Europe on May 8, 1945, to his arrival to open the office in Munich in late 1948, but much more remained untold. The stories he told—of training with MI-6 in England and visiting the Soviet Army in the Balkans, for example—were intriguing little insights into his complex life, but he gave few details about his actual activities.

Notable to me were his constant movement throughout the areas to which he was accredited, his attendance at mass at a Catholic church in each new city, and his appreciation of the art and culture of each area. When traveling he stayed in the best hotels, ate in the best restaurants, and met a stream of attractive young women of various nationalities. Val lived first class. Yet he was careful about money and saved by deducting from every paycheck an amount to invest in U.S. Treasury bonds.

MI-6, May 1945 to 1946

As the end of the war came in May 1945, Val was in England assigned to duty with MI-6. Together with British officers, jeeps, and drivers he raced through French and German territory taken by the Allied forces in search of German scientists, technicians, military leaders, or political figures wanted by the Allies for their abilities, for their knowledge of German research in fields of military interest, or because they were suspected war crimes perpetrators. Speed was essential lest the targets disappear or be captured by the Russians. His diary shows that he traveled extensively during this period through western Germany, with several multiday returns to London and multiday visits to Paris, Berlin, and Prague in 1945 and the first months of 1946. There are, unfortunately, no details about his activities.

As Naval Attaché Prague, Belgrade, and Warsaw, April 1946–June 1948

His MI-6 connection was undoubtedly ended and his duties changed when he was appointed a naval attaché in April 1946. On May 5, he flew to Paris. The entry in his travel diary for Monday May 6, 1946, reads, "Paris" and "Visas," and an intriguing, unexplained entry for Tuesday, May 7 (still at Paris) reads, "Peace Conference—Molotov–Vyshinsky."

On Wednesday, May 8, 1946, Val left Paris for Berlin and from there continued by air, train, and car through Germany and Austria to Belgrade, Zagreb, Ljubljana, Vienna, and Prague. The spare notations in his diary establish that his status as a naval attaché ended in May 1948, when he returned by ship to the United States and reported to the Office of Naval Intelligence (ONI) in Washington for assignment to his life's next adventure.

United Nations Palestine Mission, June-July 1948

On June 2, 1948, Val arrived at ONI in Washington, D.C., where he received temporary additional duty orders to serve as a military observer with the United Nations mission in Palestine/Israel headed by Count Bernadotte of Sweden. Val left by air for the Middle East on June 8, 1948, and arrived in Haifa on June 11, just as the truce began.

Later Val told me that the Palestine mission was an entirely frustrating experience because neither side wanted peace except on its own terms. Both sides made promises and neither side kept them. With wry humor Val said, "The most dangerous place in Palestine was inside a vehicle flying the blue flag of the United Nations, for both sides fired at it." He departed a month later, on July 8, 1948, aboard an aircraft carrier to Rhodes, and then he returned, by various flights, to Washington, D.C., on July 17, 1948. The rest of July and August and half of September were spent making his report at ONI and on leave in the United States.

Possart Platz 3, Munich, 1948–60

On September 14, 1948, Val left the Naval Air Training Center in Patuxent River, Maryland, on a Military Air Transport flight to Frankfurt. He arrived in Frankfurt on September 16, 1948, and then made several extensive trips by car, sometimes with others, throughout Bavaria, probably in connection with establishing the intelligence office in Munich.

Val began work on his most important accomplishments of his Navy career in late 1948, when he opened the Naval Intelligence office at Munich, and continued this work for about twelve years, until 1960. During these critical Cold War years, he recruited outstanding German personnel, including Max Parnitzki, Karl Hetz, Helmuth Pich, George Straimer, Waldtraut Sellschopp, and Toni Kinshofer, to work in the office. His team carried out a large number of interrogations of displaced persons or other border crossers from the Soviet bloc. Its productivity was very high. The office served also as a cover for and foundation for Val's other important activities.

During his time in Munich, Val also established close relations with former German general Reinhard Gehlen and his intelligence organization at Pullach. Thereby he obtained the intelligence output of the largest and most experienced intelligence organization directed at the Soviet bloc and especially at the Soviet Union's armed forces.

For many of his years in Munich, he managed a team, originally under the cover name Naval Historical Team, of former German Navy admirals who were planning the future German Navy. The leaders of this group became the advisers to Chancellor Adenauer on naval affairs, then the top commanders of the new German Navy and high-ranking officers in NATO. His work and theirs helped bring Germany into alliance with the NATO powers. And through his close involvement with the German admirals he had access to the inside thinking and politics of Germany's rearmament.

Val also established close contact with the former German Army officers employed by the Gehlen Organization who became the military advisers to Chancellor Adenauer and the top commanders of the new German Army and who also held high positions in NATO. He helped coordinate the work of the former admirals with that of these generals.

He organized a series of trips for high-ranking German intelligence and military officers to the U.S. Sixth Fleet in the Mediterranean. He personally escorted the German guests aboard major aircraft carriers, as guests of the captains, to observe fleet maneuvers demonstrating U.S. mobility and power. The German visitors were impressed by what they saw and encouraged in their efforts to bring Germany into the NATO alliance.

He recruited and supported Dr. George Straimer, a German scientist who was close to Franz Josef Strauss, head of the Christian Social Union Party and, later, defense minister in Chancellor Adenauer's government. Through Dr. Straimer, Val was able to report important information about Federal Republic politics.

He also maintained close relations with James Critchfield, the chief of the CIA's team supporting and monitoring the Gehlen Organization, and he accomplished various cooperative efforts with him.

Throughout all of these activities and accomplishments, Val forged friendships with Critchfield, General Gehlen, the former Navy admirals, and his colleagues in Possart Platz 3, and these friendships endured beyond the term of his Navy service in Munich.

The year I served in Munich was pivotal, and Val Rychly, my commanding officer, mentor, and friend, is at the center of my recollections of that time. His accomplishments were extraordinary, and by following Jack Alberti's advice to watch, listen, keep an open mind, and use my imagination, I learned lessons important to me for the rest of my life. Val was cautious in all he did. He never once held anything like a formal briefing for me, and he observed the rule of need to know. My education in the activities of the office came gradually. He revealed more and more to me and gave me more and more responsibility as he came to have confidence in me.

Last Years of Navy Active Duty: Retirement Plan

Val had twenty years of active duty service in the Navy by 1962 and could retire with a Navy pension. He decided to retire in Germany, in Neu Grünwald, a beautiful suburb at the southern edge of Munich adjacent to the Grünwald, a forest legacy to the people of Bavaria from their former royal rulers. It was a natural decision for he had spent most of his life in Europe and more than a decade in Munich. Moreover, he had likely discussed his future with Jim Critchfield and thought he might further serve his country by staying in contact with his sources and continuing his work with the CIA.

Frau Mattheus decided to stay with him in his retirement and continue to run the household. As she told me, "Val took me in after the war when I had lost everything and had nowhere to go. He gave me back my dignity and a useful role in running his household. I won't leave him when he retires." She told me later that her brother, who had rebuilt his fortune as a hotel owner in Frankfurt, had died and left her a considerable legacy, enough to buy, with Val, a large lot in Neu Grünwald and build a house on it. Indeed they bought the lot and started construction of the house in 1958 or 1959 but stopped when, in 1960, Val received orders changing his duty station from Munich to Chicago. Val and Frau Mattheus went to Chicago in 1960 and stayed until Val retired in 1962.

Val told me later that in Chicago he was assigned to interviewing travelers returning from visits behind the Iron Curtain.

Shocking Events in Chicago

I visited Val in Chicago in late January 1962. The Skipper and Frau
Mattheus met me at the airport, greeted me warmly, and took me to
their apartment. After dinner we sat down to talk, and a story of shock-
ing recent events came out.

Val had been ordered to report to the Navy hospital at the Great
Lakes Naval Station for a physical exam. To his surprise he was admit-
ted to the hospital for what he was told were standard medical tests.
The testing lasted a number of days, and although he was told that all
the tests found no problems, he was not discharged. Instead, he was
moved to the psychiatric ward supposedly "for observation." By then
he was quite suspicious of what was happening, but he could not leave
the hospital until a Navy medical officer in command released him.

It was clear that someone in authority was exerting pressure to
keep Val in the hospital. Frau Mattheus was so concerned that she
appealed to the German ambassador in Washington for help, but she
received no assistance. Finally, the Navy doctor in command of the
hospital personally intervened, found that there was no medical or
psychiatric reason to hold Val, and ordered his immediate release from
the hospital.

The Skipper and Frau Mattheus were naturally very upset by the
forced hospitalization, and they were further concerned when they
learned that Val was under investigation by the Navy based on undis-
closed suspicions or allegations. They eventually learned or deduced
that the reason for the suspicion was the house they were building in
Neu Grünwald. Someone aware of their plan to build the house who
thought that no one could afford to build a house in Neu Grünwald
on savings from Navy pay suspected that Val had embezzled Navy
funds in his control or that he had been employed as a spy by a foreign
nation. Such a suspicion could perhaps be justified if the source of the
money invested in the house were secret, but in this case it was not.
Val and Frau Mattheus spoke openly about her inheritance and their
plan for the house in Neu Grünwald. They told me, among many
others.

The Navy investigated the sources of the money that would pay for
the house in Neu Grünwald and confirmed Frau Mattheus's inheritance from her brother in the public records in Germany. The investigation was closed and Val was completely exonerated. According to
Hannelore Rychly, Val received an apology from the Navy.

Where did the suspicions or allegations against Val Rychly originate?

Val had support in high places, but many of his supporters had retired and his cooperation with Jim Critchfield and CIA was controversial among some "turf-conscious" Navy officers. Undoubtedly some of his Navy colleagues envied Val's "perks": a beautiful mansion for offices, a large house for his residential quarters, a twelve-year—as opposed to the more usual one- or two-year—tour of duty in Munich. These, and suspicions bred by the secrecy surrounding Val's activities, were fertile grounds for envy.

Retirement in Neu Grünwald

Val retired from active duty in the Navy in 1962. He and Frau Mattheus went back to Germany and finished the construction of the house at 29 Portenländer Strasse in Neu Grünwald. It was a gracious house that combined the modern and the traditional in a pleasing way, indicative of the owners' personalities and experiences. The kitchen and bathrooms were modern, but the other spaces were furnished with traditional, elegant, sometimes antique furniture. Oriental carpets covered the floors, valuable paintings adorned the walls, and Val kept his treasured violin on display. Both Frau Mattheus and the Skipper were conservative in their tastes, but Frau Mattheus had more than just aesthetic reasons for her purchases. As she explained to me during my first visit to their home, twice in her lifetime German money had lost all its value so she now invested only in tangible, useful, and beautiful things and in gold. She looked back with approval on the stable pre-World War I days of "*der gute, alte Kaiser*" (the good, old Kaiser). Val had a keen artistic sense, appreciated fine things, and set a high standard in all his possessions. When I was serving with him in Munich, he drove a black Jaguar, and when I visited him after his retirement, the car in the garage was a new black Mercedes sedan.

In 1963 Frau Mattheus's granddaughter, Hannelore, moved into the house to take care of her elderly grandmother. Hannelore brought her smiles, gourmet cooking, bountiful love, and caring to the household. In 1972 Val and Hannelore were married. At the time, Frau Mattheus, ever practical, told me that she had urged Val and Hannelore to marry "to keep the property in the family." From what I saw when visiting, Cupid had also done his work; the affection between them was true.

CIA Contract

Since his days as naval attaché in the Balkans, Val had been a friend of

Jim Critchfield, who was at that time head of U.S. Army Intelligence in Austria, and they had exchanged information about areas of their mutual interest.[1] Thereafter, at Munich, Val and Jim Critchfield, then chief of the CIA's Gehlen Organization group at Pullach, worked cooperatively. Their close professional and personal connection continued after Val's Navy retirement.

I can't help thinking that Val had sources inside the Gehlen Organization who told him about things happening within the organization that the CIA did not know about. Based on stories Val told me and dinner guests I met at his house, I formed a strong impression that several Gehlen Organization officers were very close to Val and supplied him with important information.

Val Rychly's service to the United States did not end with his retirement. It took a little while to work things out, but the CIA contracted Val for his services for a number of years.

Jim Critchfield, who became the head of the CIA's Near East Division in the early 1960s, visited the Rychlys frequently. Val and Critchfield continued their important work together, but they were more than professional colleagues, they were devoted friends. Each of them was, moreover, independently a friend of Gen. Reinhard Gehlen. The ties binding all three and their families were shown by the reunion of General Gehlen's children, Jim Critchfield and his wife, and Val's widow Hannelore at the Rychlys' house in May 1998, years after the deaths of General Gehlen (1979) and Val Rychly (1992).

Rychly's Death

CDR Vladimir L. Rychly, USNR, died of a heart attack in November 1992 at age eighty-three. Frau Mattheus died shortly thereafter, at age ninety-eight. They rest peacefully in *Waldfriedhof Grünwald* (Grünwald Forest Cemetery). Val's widow Hannelore has since sold their house, and the buyers knocked it down to build a much larger house. Hannelore lives in a smaller place in Grünwald, still near the forest.

Recognition of Service

Gehlen, Critchfield, and Rychly—together with the former admirals and generals with whom they worked—helped bring Germany into

---

1. James H. Critchfield, *Partners at the Creation: The Men Behind Postwar Germany's Defense and Intelligence Establishments* (Annapolis, MD: Naval Institute Press, 2003), 103.

the North Atlantic alliance of free and democratic nations and influenced the course of history. In his book *Partners at the Creation*, Critchfield writes, "Rychly can be credited with an important contribution in the history of the transition of the German Navy from an enemy to a member of the Allied Fleet."[2]

In recognition of Val Rychly's service in the creation of a democratic Germany allied to the West, the government of the Federal Republic awarded him the *Bundes Verdienstkreuz*—the new Germany's highest decoration, awarded for military or other service. According to his widow, Hannelore Rychly, he was the first American to be so honored.

---

2. Critchfield, *Partners at the Creation*, 103–104.

EPILOGUE

I am seventy-eight years old. Almost all of my friends or colleagues from my year with Naval Intelligence in Munich have passed away. Possart Strasse and Possart Platz can no longer be found on a Munich city map; they have been renamed Shakespeare Strasse and Shakespeare Platz. But the beautiful big house I knew as Possart Platz 3 still stands, still looks out over the wooded park-like square in Bogenhausen. And my memories of the year 1955–56 in Munich have not dimmed; they are as vivid as if the events had happened yesterday.

My term of active duty in the Navy expired in February 1956. I received my orders in December 1955:

23 December 1955

From: Commander, U.S. Naval Forces Germany
To: LTJG Marvin B. Durning, 474092/1105 USNR
Subj: Release from active duty

. . . When directed by Commander, U.S. Naval Forces, Germany on or about 1 February 1956, you will regard yourself detached from duty on the Staff of Commander, U.S. Naval Forces, Germany and from such other duty as may have been assigned you. . . . You will proceed to a port in the United States and upon arrival further proceed immediately and report to the nearest appropriate activity for temporary duty in connection with your separation processing. . . .

The trip was long: I traveled from Munich to Heidelberg by train; I had my orders endorsed at COMNAVGER in Heidelberg and made a courtesy call to the admiral to say good-bye; I took a bus to

Rhein-Main Air Force Base and then a flight over the Atlantic to Maguire Air Force Base in New Jersey; and finally I took a Navy bus to the Philadelphia Navy Yard for the processing of my release from active duty.

During this long trip I had much time to think about my year of duty in Munich, and I recognized that I might never again learn so much so quickly or be so closely involved in matters of such importance as Germany's future, with its implications for Europe and the world. I recognized also that I was fortunate to have been sent to Germany during such an interesting period, and I realized that my situation in 1955–56 was very different from the experience of the soldiers who had fought there in World War II and the conditions of officers and men in Korea or on U.S. Navy ships spread across the world's oceans. I recognized that Fortune had smiled on me, and I was grateful for the gift.

Matryoshka and Possart Platz 3

Some years ago, during Mikhail Gorbachev's presidency, the period of perestroika and glasnost, I visited the Soviet Union. Politics and government were changing rapidly in Russia, but some aspects of Russian culture had remained constant. One of these was Russian love of traditional *matryoshka* (little mother) dolls. Made of wood, the dolls were painted in bright colors, with shiny black eyes, a multicolored and flowered headscarf, and a small red enigmatically smiling mouth. Each doll was hollow and cut at the waist so that the top half could be taken off to reveal a smaller matryoshka inside and an even smaller doll inside of that. There were six dolls in total. When all were assembled and nested one inside the other, there was only one doll. Each doll provided cover for the next: a matrushka is a treasury of secrets.

I bought several matryoshkas for my grandchildren and one for myself. My matryoshka sits on my desk as I write this. As I recall my time working with the Skipper at Possart Platz 3, I think of a big matrushka holding many secrets inside, each covering for another. The largest matryoshka was the intelligence office at Possart Platz 3, which received, translated, and forwarded the Gehlen Organization's reports about the Soviet bloc to the Office of Naval Intelligence. These activities, very important in themselves, also provided cover for Commander Rychly's highly secret work with the German admirals who were planning a new German Navy. If you removed the top of the first matryoshka, you would find this second. But the second matryoshka covered a third: the Skipper's work with the former German admirals and former German generals, for example, Generals Heusinger and Speidel, as well as General Gehlen, including providing the officers with influential trips to the U.S. Sixth Fleet's aircraft carriers in the Mediterranean to observe the power and mobility of the U.S. Navy. Removing the top of the third we find a fourth matryoshka: Dr. Straimer's scientific and political activities in Bavaria and the Federal Republic. If the top were removed from that fourth matryoshka, another would be found: the operations Rychly worked on with Critchfield, for which I was a courier. There may have been more matryoshkas inside, but any other activities were unknown to me.

Success: The World Turned Upside Down

In the years following my return to the United States I stayed in touch with the Skipper, with Max and Waldtraut, and with Helmuth. Our ties did not weaken; they grew stronger as we all looked back at those memorable days in Munich. Led by Val Rychly and working in common cause, we had outstanding success in reaching our goals.

The first half of the twentieth century saw two world wars with Germany at the center of both. But everything changed between 1945 and 1956. The people of Germany evolved from defeated enemy to friend and ally of the Western powers. In these first years of the twenty-first century, a time of criticism of U.S. intelligence agencies, it is important to recognize the success of the U.S. Army, CIA, and U.S. Naval Intelligence in the Cold War struggle over Germany's future.

There have been many dangerous events in the half-century since 1956, including the Soviet crushing of uprisings in Hungary and Czechoslovakia; the building of the Berlin Wall in 1961 and its removal in 1989; the wars in Korea, Vietnam, and the Balkans; the continuing crisis of Israel and its neighbors; the Gulf War in Kuwait and Iraq; the present fighting in Afghanistan and Iraq and the war on terrorism. The Western alliance has endured many strains, none greater than the differences over the present fighting in Iraq. But the basic alliance with Germany that was formed in 1956 has held.

For fifty years since 1956 there has been no war in western Europe, and the reunited Germany has become a respected, pluralistic, and prosperous democracy and a leading member of the European Union. The Cold War is over. The Soviet Union is no more.

In the decade after World War II the people of Germany changed; they traveled a long journey, from Nuremberg to NATO. Americans and Germans alike can be proud of the accomplishments of that decade. Those of us who worked with Val Rychly at Possart Platz 3 can be especially proud, for we all worked hard—together—with all our wits and strength at the cutting edge of the Cold War struggle, and we and many others were rewarded by success: a stable peace in Europe—the world turned upside down.

APPENDIX A

Max Parnitzki's Brief Curriculum Vitae
and Experience as a Prisoner of War

Max Parnitzki

Brief Curriculum Vitae
and
Experience as a Prisonner of War in the USSR

1. **Brief Curriculum Vitae:** I originate from a German family, which emmigrated to Russia before the World War I but never gave up the German citizenship. Thus, even though I was born in Kharkov, USSR, in 1919, I always have been a German citizen too. In 1933 my family legally returned to Germany and settled in BERLIN. In that city I attended the Deutsch-Russisches Realgymnasium (high-school) and upon graduation enlisted in the German Army. My military career led me after the completion of basic and field training with an artillery unit in East Prussia to the signal corps and to various radio monitoring units (radio interception intelligence). In late June 1944, when the beaten 9th German Army was trying to break out of the Soviet encirclement in Byelorussia, I was wounded and taken prisonner of war by the Soviet Army. With a group of 700 to 800 wounded German POWs I was marched to a Soviet field hospital at NOVOZYBKOV.

2. **Activitiy in POW Camps:** In October or November 1944 all POW who had recovered from their wounds were transferred from the hospital to the POW camp No. 7056 in BOBRUISK. Actually this was a group of POW camps scattered in and around BOBRUISK. The largest camps of this group were located in BOBRUISK proper (Nos. 7056/1 and 7056/3) and at KAMENKA about 9 kilometers west of BOBRUISK (7056/2). I had not tried to conceal from the Russians my knowledge of their language and was therefore employed in the camp as an interpreter. My assignments during the time as a POW were as follows:

    a. **Late 1944 - May or June 1945:** Interpreter for the Soviet medical officer in charge of the camp hospital at 7056/1.

    b. **June 1945 - October 1945:** On request of another Russian medical officer, I was transferred to a small camp at GLUSHA (25 km west of BOBRUIS) and helped with a few other "old-time" POWs to set up camp facilities (kitchen, dispensary, camp joinery, workshops, etc.) for a group of prisonners, which arrived after the capitulation of Germany in the summer of 1945. This camp was organized by the Soviets to assist in the reconstruction of a glass mill. In October 1945 it was closed down and the POWs were transferred to KAMENKA (7056/2).

    c. **November 1945 - mid-1947:** I was again assigned as an interpreter to the Soviet medical officer in charge of the camp dispensary in the camp No. 7056/2.

    d. **Mid-1947 - August 1948:** When a new Soviet political indoctrianation officer (who did not speak any German) arrived in the camp at KAMENKA, he picked me up to assist him, i.e. to translate his speeches, the speeches of German so-called "anti-fascist" functionaries (POWs, who pretended to be communists and acted as political indoctrination and education instructors); to translate into Russian

163

- 2 -

articles published in German newspapers (Sovzone publications, which
were available in the camp), and articles from Russian newspapers into
Germany. Sometime in early 1948 I was transferred from the camp No
7056/2 to the camp No. 7056/1 in BOBRUISK, where I was again assigned
as an interpreter and translator to the Soviet political indoctrination officer. In August 1948 I was arrested by the Operations
Department (state security department of the camp administration) and
put into a prison outside the camp for interrogation on alleged
war crimes. I was kept in this confinement for roughly six or seven
months. (For a detailed description of this experience, see paragraphs
below). In February or early March 1949 I was released and returned
to camp No. 7056/2 at KAMENKA. I was no longer allowed to be assigned
any other activity but physical labor.

    e. June 1949 - late December 1949: In June 1949 I was transfer-
red with a group of other POWs to the camp 7168/14 in MINSK. The
prisonners of this camp were employed in the construction of a tractor
plant. I worked there as a laborer and later as a plumber on the construction site. When this camp was closed down in August 1949, the
remaining POWs, among them I, were transferred to the camp No. 7168/11
(automobile plant). Then followed transfers to camps Nos. 7168/3,
7168/6, which, however, were closed downs succesively. Finally, all
remaining POWs, who were not sentenced to hard labor for alleged
war crimes, were concentrated again in the camp No. 7168/11 and thence
dismissed to Germany in October, November, and December 1949. I was
released with the second last group on 2 January 1950.

3. Activities of the Soviet Political Indoctrination and Operations
    Departments: Apart from strictly administrative sections of the
Soviet POW camp administration, such as the labor department, supply
department, etc., there existed in each Soviet POW camp two departments, which were assigned special tasks. These were the Political
Indoctrination Department (Politotdel) headed by the deputy camp commander for political affairs, and the Operations Department (Operativ-
nyy Otdel - Otdel Gosbesopasnosti/ Operations department - state
security department), the members of which were not subordinate to
the camp commander but formed a special organization directed by
authorities of the Ministry of State Security (MGB) or the Ministry
of Home (MVD). The political indoctrination officer of the camp and
his various instructors (one to two officers per cam) were responsible
for two fields of activity: (1) the current political indoctrination
of Soviet personnel assigned to the camp, and (2) for the political
education and indoctriantion of prisonners of war. It was this department, which organized the anti-fascist movement in the camps; selected
trained, and supervised the activities of Germans, who agreed to pro-
fess communist ideas among their comrades; conducted political meeting
procured communist publications, etc. However, this department was
neither authorised nor generally attempted to carry out investigations

- 3 -

of the so-called war crimes or to enlist POWs for intelligence activities other than that of political informers. Some political officers, for instance First Lieutenant SEIDENWAHR (who was at camp
7056/1 in 1945-47 and at the camp 7168/11 during 1948 and 1949) undoubtedly cooperated with the Operations Department, however, on a
personal basis. Others, such as Sub-lieutenant PRIBYLOW at camp
7056/1 in 1948-1949 tried to confine their activities strictly to
political matters. The Operations Department xxxxxxxxxxxxx was
manned by especially trained officers of the sta e security service
of the MVD or MGB. The chief occupation of these officers in POW
camps was the investigation of what the Soviets called war crimes and
crimes against humanity committed by the members of the former Axis
forces during the war. I guess that each POW had been screened and
interrogated by the Operations Department. Many were put in special
interrogation prisons, which had been built in nearly every camp,
were brainwashed and tortured there. It was the Operations Department
that enlisted or pressed POWs (and also Russian personnel) to act as
informers. The persons who agreed to cooperated with the Operations
Department were required to sign a statement of collaboration. As
far as I know, these secret informers (many of them were known to
other prisoners in the camp though) were employed to approach suspect
war criminals and other comrades in order to induce the latter to
tell something incriminating about their war experience. Although it
is possible that the Soviets intended to use these persons as intelligence agents upon their return to Germany, I have never heard that
such future tasks had been discussed with them. Since the fate of
each POWnand his ultimate release or detention in a forced labor camp
depended on the Operations Department, it was the most feared installation in the camp. However, many prisoners did not quite realise
whether the Operations Department and the Political Indoctriantion
Department were one and the same or different organizations and therefore believed that their membership in the anti-fascist movement
could save them from troubles with the Operations Department.
4. My Personal Encounters with the Operations Department: As I have
already stated, I did not try to conceal my ability to speak Russian
and was tehrefore used as an interpreter. Already in the Soivet
hospital at NOVOZYBKOV, where I was reconvering from my wound, I was
warned by a Russian lady physician that the operations officer of
the hospital suspected me of being a Soviet renegade. She advised me
to be very coutious during future interrogations. On arrival in the
camp 7056/1 at BOBRUISK I was reuired, as all other POWs, to fill out
the standard questionnair. This paper contained fifty or sixty questio
about the place and date of birth, education, military ranks, deco-
rations, relatives in Germany and abroad as well as about the military
career and wartime assignments. I correctly answered them but reduced
the description of my military career to a few general statements.

- 4 -

In the summer of 1946 I was summoned by the Operations Officer in
the camp 7056/2 and ordered to fill out the same questionnaire again.
However, in the meantime most POWs have discovered that it was dangerous to mention certain war assignements such as anti-guerilla
opsrations, participation in the evacuation of civilian population
from the combat zone, not to speak of actions that were openly declared to be war crimes (blowing up of bridges, destruction of
buildings, etc.). I therefore tailored my statements about the military career, omitting the fact that I had been assigned to combat
guerillas in the summer of 1942 and 1943. On the ohter hand I was
certain that even Russians could not accuse a boy of 14 (the age when
I left Russia in 1933) and did not hesitate to give information on
the place and date of my birth (1919, KHARKOV) as well as the date of
our departure from Russia. Next time, I believe it was in May or
June 1947,I was again summoned to the office of the operations officer and interrogated in detail on my military career. The interrogation was conducted by the chief operations officer of the camp
7056, Lieutenant Colonel KRUGLIKOV. Apparently the Soviets had
accepted my previous statements and did not find any cues. KRUGLIKOV
interrogated, his assistant (I forget his name) recorded my statements in writing. I insisted tha my radio intelligence platoon did
nothing but to intercept Soviet coded radio messages and forward
these recordings to the company staff (from letters of my mother I
knew that the company CO had escaped captivity) but did not officially
know what happened to them. KRUGLIKOV in turn tried to extract of me
a statement that these documents were intended for the division or
army intelligence departments and wanted me to acknowledge my cooperation with these departments. I knew by that time that the field-
intelligence personnel were regarded as war criminals too and therefore refused to admit any direct cooperation with the intelligence
departments. Thus the interrogation ended without an apparent dis-
advantage to me. Suddenly, in August 1948, I was arrested and put
in a cell of the camp prison at BOBRUISK. The first interrogation
was very general. The Soviet officer simply accused me of being a
monster, a war criminal, a bandit, and urged me to make a full con-
fession. I naturally denied all these accusations. Until January
1949 I was left in the prison but no charges were brought forth against
me.

        In January 1949, I was fetched out of the cell at midnight and
conducted to the office of Lieutenant-Colonel KRUGLIKOV. He and his
deputy, Captain KARSANOV, attempted to enlist me as an informer.
Contrary to previous interrogations, when I was required to stand at
attention, this time I was allowed to sit down, was offered a cigaret
asked whether I got enough to eat, all this apparently to place me
in a complacent mood. In the following I shall try to reproduce
the basic elements of the ensuing conversation:

- 5 -

KRUGLIKOV: Are you a member of the anti-fascist movement in the camp?

I: Yes. (As 95 % of all POW I had agreed to join this so-called movement to avoid discrimination).

KR.: So you are an anti-fascist!

I: Yes, I am.

KR.: How do you prove this?

I: I do not know, how a man can prove his political convictions, except that he professes them to other people.

KR.: No, this is not enough. A faithful anti-fascist (read: communist) takes an active part in the fight between the proletariate and the capitalists and fascists. He keeps his eyes open, tears down the masks from fascist faces, and takes the poison from their fangs. In the camp, a true anti-fascist helps us to detect the fascists.

I: But if there are fascists, they do not tell so in public. I know no one in the camp.

KR.: This is because you did not care to detect them. Would your report one, if you knew a person to be a fascist?

I: I think, I would.

KR.: Now, I shall give you a chance to prove your loyalty to the anti-fascist cause. But first go over to the other office with Captain KARSANOV and finish the formalities.

I: What formalities?

KR.: Well, you just will sign a paper stating that you will collaborate with us.

I: But what for? I am a German and if I sign any such statements I shall be treated as a spy at home.

KR.: You are wrong. In our common fight of the proletariate against the capitalists, there exist no countries and borders. You may return to the German Democratic Republic and continue our fight there.

I: But look, Colonel, what if you discover that a Soviet citizen is an agent of the Polish government?

KR.: We shall treat him as a traitor. (This was a slip!).

I: You see, the same will happen to me in Germany. Poland is a people's democracy too. I shall not sign any papers.

KR.: Then you are a fascist yourself!

I: No, I am not, but I do not want to sign any obligations of co-operation with you.

KR.: Alright! Never mind! If you are an anti-fascist, as you say, you will have to prove it. There are fascists in your neighborhood; they are in the same cell with you (he named Lt.Col.Hermann OFFENBECHER and the Fst.Lieut. NIETZKI, who were confined in the same cell with me). You are chums; they will tell you their crimes, if you want them to. And beware, we know each word that you speak in the cell. Do not try to doublecross us! Now go!

- 6 -

Upon my return into the cell, I stealthily informed all concerned
about what KRUGLIKOV wanted me to do. We had a mate in our cell, whom
we suspected to be an informer, and naturally communicated, when he
could not hear us. We decided that I could repeat, when summoned
again, a summary of statements, which my comrades (NIETZKI and
OFFENBECHER) had made themselves during interrogations. However,
when I was actually summoned by KARSANOV and started repeating what
we had agreed to say, the Russian exploded, called me a scoundrel,
a fascist, promised that I should never see Germany again, would be
sent to VORKUTA, and finally ordered a guard to put me in the kennel:
a ply-board cabinet about 70 x 70 cm large and 190 high, which stood
in a cold room of the building. After four days, during which I never
left this kennel, KARSANOV once again asked if I was willing to
cooperate. I answered that I could tell no more and do no more then
I did. He threatened me again but ordered that I be returned into
the cell. After that I have not been interrogated again, was transferred with a few other inmates to the ᵡᵢᵡᵢᵡᵢᵡᵢᵡᵢᵡᵢᵡᵢᵡᵢᵡᵢᵡ camp
prison at KAMENKA (7056/2) and after another six weeks released into
the camp. Before release I was required to sign a statement of
promise that I shall never speak about what I saw or heard in the
prison.
The Soviet operaᵢons department never again attempted to enlist me as
an informer or agent. The only retaliation for my refusal to cooperat
was the order to assign me to hard work. As a matter of face, I
did not feel like a hero during the interrogations; I was very
scared. I found the strength to resist, since I knew that any
committment on my part would ruin my life, if and when the Soviets
may release me to go home.
Here is a list of persons (whom I remember) who were with me in the
prison and would cooraborate my statements:
1. Rudi SCHUETT, employee of the labor office at KONSTANZ.
    Address: KONSTANZ a. Bodensee, Schobuliweg 8.
2. Hermann OFFENBECHER, vocational school teacher by profession,
    ex Lt.Col. of the German army. His present whereabouts are un-
    known to me. He used to live at either FRANKFURT/M. or WIESBA-
    DEN. I heard, he returned from Russia in 1955 or 1956.
3. NIETZKI, fnu., lawyer by profession, from KOENIGSBERG. His
    family lived after 1945 somewhere near HANNOVER.
4. Theo ZIEBART. He returned to German in late December 1949 and
    lived with his father somewhere near NORTHEIM or WOLFENBUETTEL.
Other former POW, hwo knew me in the camps 7056 and 7168 and may
be inquired about my attitude in the camp:
1. Dr.Heinz SCHWEITZER, DUESEELDORF, Grupellostr. 14.
2. Kurt SHUFERT, BERLIN-FRIEDENAU, Grazer Damm 197.
3. Karl-Ernst KRUEGER, BREMEN, Hardenbergstr. 51.
4. Dr. Sigismund BERGMEISTER, PFAFFENHOFEN/ILM, Auerstr.38.
5. Ferdinand ALTENA, STOLLBERG, Rathausstr. 87.

APPENDIX B

Max Parnitzki's Iron Cross

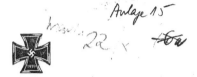

Im Namen des Führers und Oberſten Befehlshabers der Wehrmacht

verleihe ich

dem

Uffz. Maximilian Parnitzky

5./Pz.Gr.Nachr.Rgt.2

das

Eiſerne Kreuz 2. Klaſſe.

Gef.St. Tolotschin, den 13. Juli 1941.

(Dienſtſiegel)

Generaloberſt und
Befehlshaber der Panzergruppe 2

(Dienſtgrad und Dienſtſtellung)

APPENDIX C

U.S. Navy Letter of Recommendation for Max Parnitzki

Representative, Munich
c/o U. S. Consulate
APO 108, U. S. Forces
New York, N. Y.

1 April 1962

To Whom It May Concern

It is with great pleasure that I give the highest personnal and professional recommendations to Mr. Maximilian Parnitzki, an employee of this organization from 4 February 1952 to 1 April 1962. Mr. Parnitzki's fluency in several languages, including English and Russian, has been a most valuable asset to this activity. His duties, as supervisory military intelligence research analyst consisted of the preparation of studies of maritime and naval problems and the professional evaluation of maritime and naval matters. In addition, he supervised the translation and research activities of several employees, competently and efficiently.

Mr. Parnitzki displayed the highest qualities of leadership and demonstrated exceptional knowledge of his assignments carrying them out with maximum effectiveness. His astuteness, keen judgement, knowledgeability and capacity for original and professional work is most favorably reflected in his outstanding performance.

The employment of Mr. Parnitzki is terminated with the deepest regret. He leaves with our best wishes for continued success in his new position with the Presse-und Informationsamt der Bundesregierung.

Chester J. Slemiacz
Commander, U. S. Navy

170

APPENDIX D

Letter from Undersecretary of Navy to Val Rychly

THE UNDER SECRETARY OF THE NAVY
WASHINGTON

25 July 1955

Dear Commander:

I hope you will forgive the delay in writing you to thank you for the very great help you were to us on our recent trip to Germany. Without your assistance at Garmisch, we would have had considerable difficulty in that area; with your help, our stay in Germany was as delightful as any single part of our trip.

The arrangements you made for us on our arrival at Munich, our visit at Garmisch and our trip to Heidelberg were superb. It was particularly nice to be able to tour Munich with you and Lieutenant Durning, and in this brief time to get to know the two of you better. I imagine your duty there in Munich is among the most interesting in the whole United States Navy. It must be a very challenging job.

Our trip to Garmisch and on to Heidelberg was something we will all of us remember. We took Lt. Durning's and your advice in what we saw and can only say it lived up to all your promises. It was unfortunate that the other members of our party were delayed a day, for they certainly missed one of the loveliest spots in this world. For myself, I intend to return to Garmisch some day with Mrs. Gates to show her that very beautiful country.

Again, thanks a million to you and Lt. Durning for having taken such good care of us. With best personal regards.

Sincerely yours,

LCdr. V. L. Rychly, USNR
c/o Commander Naval Forces, Germany
APO #403
c/o Postmaster
New York, N. Y.

APPENDIX E

Two Pages from Val L. Rychly's Travel Diary (1946)

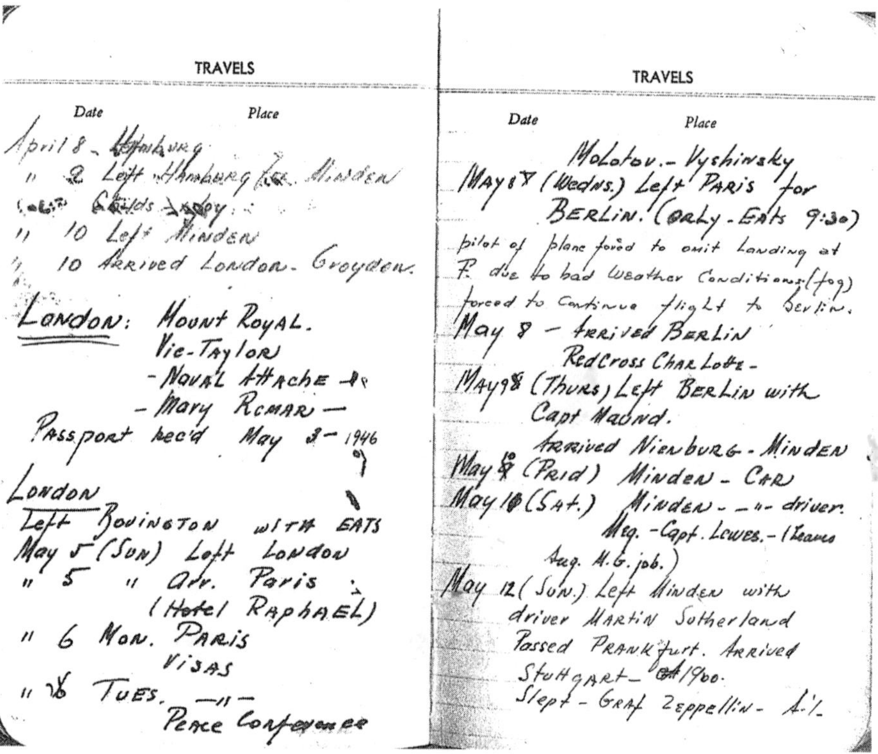

TRAVELS

Date Place

April 8 - Hamburg
" 9 Left Hamburg for Minden
Childs
" 10 Left Minden
" 10 Arrived London - Croydon.

London: Mount Royal.
Vic-Taylor
- Naval Attache
- Mary Rcmar -
Passport rec'd May 3 - 1946

London
Left Bovington with Eats
May 5 (Sun) Left London
" 5 " Arr. Paris
(Hotel Raphael)
" 6 Mon. Paris
Visas
" 7 Tues. —"—
Peace Conference

TRAVELS

Date Place

Molotov. - Vyshinsky
May 8 (Weds.) Left Paris for
Berlin. (Orly - Eats 9:30)
pilot of plane forced to omit landing at
F. due to bad weather conditions (fog)
forced to continue flight to Berlin.
May 8 - Arrived Berlin
RedCross Charlotte -
May 9 (Thurs) Left Berlin with
Capt Maund.
Arrived Nienburg - Minden
May 10 (Frid) Minden - Car
May 11 (Sat.) Minden - " - driver.
Meg. - Capt. Lowes. - (leaves
Aug. M.G. job.)
May 12 (Sun.) Left Minden with
driver Martin Sutherland
Passed Frankfurt. Arrived
Stuttgart - at 1900.
Slept - Graf Zeppelin - A.1.

Date	Place
	Han Pijesak (Romania)
July 31 -	Left Belgrade via Šabac-Loznice-Zvornik
July 31 -	Arr. Sarajevo - Ungert - B. is Secr.
	of Sir
	paid # 675 for 100 l. of gas
Aug 1 -	Left Sarajevo. Mostar. Imotsko Split -
" 1 -	Arrive Split - Stay Hotel Bellevue
" 2 =	Split - Mr. Harvey.
" 3 -	" " "
" 4 -	" " ".
" 5 -	Leave Split - via Omiš, Makarska - Metkovie
" 5 -	Arrive Dubrovnik - Villa Argentina -
" 6 -	Mr. Pribram - (4 cans gas) Brothers Zuanic
" 7 -	Dubrovnik - Opera Singer -
" 8 -	Dubrovnik - Nana
" 9 -	Leave Dubrovnik - via Castat, Cibri,
	Ercegnovi - T - Budva (Mr. P. Stipanic)
" 9 -	Arrive Budva
" 10 -	Budva - Medusa
" 11 -	Budva
" 12 -	Leave Budva - via T - Ferry boat
	to Dubrovnik

Date	Place
Aug 12 -	Arrive Dubrovnik - Villa Argentina
" 13 -	Dubrovnik
" 14 -	Leave Dubrovnik - via Metkovié, Mostar,
	Jablanica, Konjic to Sarajevo - 3 Hotel
	Hotel Europa - Moslem district
" 15 -	Leave Sarajevo - Mr. n Mos. Konvig.
" 15 -	Arrive Belgrade - 8 flats
" 16 -	Belgrade
" 17 -	Belgrade
" 18 -	Belgrade
" 19 -	Belgrade
" 20 -	Belgrade
" 21 -	Belgrade
" 22 -	Belgrade
" 23 -	Belgrade (Fri.) Left Belgrade via
	Czech Air (Douglass) Arrive Praha 14:00
Fri - Aug. 23	Alcron Hotel - Praha
Aug. 24. (Sat.)	Praha
" 25 (Sun.)	Outing with Č-Š vicinity of Praha
" 25 (Mon)	Celakovice - Eve. 2 denek
" 26 (Tues)	Praha - Eve. lob. St. by Prenuell

GLOSSARY

Abitur the exam students in Germany take to qualify for university entrance

Abwehr a German intelligence service eliminated by Hitler in 1944

Amt Blank Office headed by Theodor Blank, precursor to West German Defense Ministry

Alle/Alles all, everything

Anschluss annexation

Bayer a person from Bavaria

Bayerisch Bavarian dialect

Bier beer

bitte please

Blitzkrieg lightning war

BOQ bachelor officers quarters

Bundes Presse- und Informationsamt Federal Press and Information Office

Bundeskanzleramt office of the chancellor of the Federal Republic

Bundesmarine Federal Navy (of West Germany)

Bundesrepublik Deutschland Federal Republic of Germany (West Germany)

Bundestag lower house of parliament of Federal Republic of Germany

Bundeswehr armed forces of the Federal Republic of Germany

CDU Christian Democratic Union, the more conservative of West Germany's two major political parties

CIC U.S Army Counter-Intelligence Corps

CINCNELM U.S Commander-in-Chief Northeast Atlantic and Mediterranean

CNO U.S Chief of Naval Operations
COMNAVGER U.S Commander Naval Forces, Germany
CSU Christian Social Union, the largest political party in Bavaria

danke thank you
Deutsche Demokratische Republik (DDR) German Democratic Republic (East Germany)
Dirndl short-sleeved, low-necked dress with a tight embroidered bodice and a gathered skirt, the traditional Bavarian woman's costume
DNI U.S Director of Naval Intelligence

FLOGWING U.S Navy Fleet Logistic Air Wing
Fremde Heere Ost Foreign Armies East (FHO), a part of German Army General Staff
Führer leader, used as title for Hitler
Funkbeobachtung radio intercepts and monitoring

Gaststätte restaurant or tavern
gemütlich comfortable, friendly, cozy (there is no exact translation)
Gemütlichkeit that which makes something *gemütlich*
General Staff elite organization in the German Army famed for thorough and precise planning
Gestapo Geheime Staatspolizei, the Nazi secret state police, organized in 1933 by Goering and ultimately controlled by the SS.
Guten Abend good evening
Guten Morgen good morning

Hausmeister caretaker of household, janitor

Junker Prussian landed aristocracy

KGB Soviet State Security Committee, a Soviet intelligence agency
Kriegsdienst war service
Kriegsgefangener prisoner of war
Kriegsmarine Germany's World War II Navy

Lederhosen leather shorts with suspenders, the traditional Bavarian man's costume
Leutnant Lieutenant
Luftwaffe German air force

Marshall Plan an American multibillion dollar program of economic assistance for war-torn European countries named for Gen. George C. Marshall, then–secretary of state, who proposed it on behalf of President Truman.

MATS U.S Military Air Transport Service

MI-6 British Secret Intelligence Service

München Munich

NHT Naval Historical Team, a U.S Navy-supported group of former German Navy officers

ONI U.S Office of Naval Intelligence

OSS U.S Office of Strategic Services, World War II precursor to CIA

Ostfront East Front

Ostheer German Army on the East Front

Panzer German Army tank

Polizeidienststelle police station

Reichsarbeitsdienst national labor service

Reichswehr pre-Hitler German Army

RSHA *Reichssicherheitshauptamt*, Head Office for Reich Security, a Nazi organization

S&T Science and technology intelligence branch of ONI

Schnellboote or *S-boote* (S-boats) fast German World War II boats similar to American PT boats

Sicherheitsdienst (SD) Security Service, the intelligence and espionage arm of the Nazi SS.

Schutzstaffel (SS) armed Nazi paramilitary organization created in 1929 and expanded ultimately into a Nazi Party fourth armed service, responsible among other things for carrying out the "Final Solution," i.e., the Holocaust.

Sommer Denkschrift summer "Think Piece"

Strasse street

TAD Temporary Additional Duty (U.S Navy)

USNR U.S Navy Reserve

Das Vaterland the Fatherland

Waffen SS elite Nazi Party army developed from the SS
Wehrdienst military defense service
Wehrmacht German armed forces
Wiederheimkehrer repatriated prisoner(s) of war
Wirtschaftswunder economic miracle

yeoman in the U.S. Navy, a sailor whose specialty is typing and
administrative and clerical tasks

SELECTED BIBLIOGRAPHY

M any books and articles in German and in English cover Germany in the years after World War II. Some of the books have extensive bibliographies. I have read widely among these sources but found that only a few in English have information about the U.S.-sponsored Gehlen Organization, and none describe the role of U.S. Naval Intelligence or the activities of Commander Vladimir Rychly. Three books address the secret Gehlen Organization: Mary Ellen Reese's *General Reinhard Gehlen: The CIA Connection*; James Critchfield's *Partners at the Creation*; and Gen. Reinhard Gehlen's memoir, *The Service*. Dr. Douglas Peifer's recent book, *The Three German Navies*, tells of some early postwar U.S. Navy activities but does not cover the activities of U.S. Naval Intelligence in Munich under Commander Rychly.

Acheson, Dean. *Present at the Creation: My Years at the State Department.* New York: Norton, 1969.
Beevor, Antony. *The Fall of Berlin, 1945.* New York: Penguin Books, 2002.
———. *Stalingrad: The Fateful Siege, 1942–1943.* New York: Penguin Books, 1998.
Bury, J. B. *The Invasion of Europe by the Barbarians.* New York: Norton, 1967.
Churchill, Winston. "Iron Curtain Speech" [actual title "Sinews of Peace"]. Westminster College, Fulton, MO, March 5, 1946. www.fordham.edu/halsall/mod/churchill-iron.html.
Critchfield, James H. *Partners at the Creation: The Men behind Postwar Germany's Defense and Intelligence Establishments.* Annapolis, MD: Naval Institute Press, 2003.

Davidson, Eugene. *The Death and Life of Germany: An Account of the American Occupation.* New York: Knopf, 1959.

Fitzgibbon, Constantine. *Denazification.* London: Michael Joseph, 1969.

Gehlen, Reinhard. *The Service: The Memoirs of General Reinhard Gehlen.* Translated by David Irving. New York: World Publishing, 1972.

Grosser, Alfred. *The Federal Republic of Germany: A Concise History.* Translated by Nelson Aldrich. New York: Frederick A Praeger, 1964.

Keegan, John. *The Second World War.* New York: Penguin Books, 1989.

Keesing's Research Report. *Germany and Eastern Europe since 1945: From the Potsdam Agreement to Chancellor Brandt's "Ostpolitik."* New York: Charles Scribner's Sons, 1973.

Peifer, Douglas C. *The Three German Navies.* Gainesville: University Press of Florida, 2002.

Persico, Joseph E. *Nuremberg: Infamy on Trial.* New York: Penguin Books, 1994.

Reese, Mary Ellen. *General Reinhard Gehlen: The CIA Connection.* Fairfax, VA: George Mason University Press, 1990.

Shirer, William F. *The Rise and Fall of the Third Reich.* New York: Simon & Schuster, 1960.

Smyser, W. R. *From Yalta to Berlin: The Cold War Struggle over Germany.* New York: St. Martin's Griffin, 1999.

Tipton, Frank B. *A History of Modern Germany since 1815.* Berkeley: University of California Press, 2003.

Tuchman, Barbara. *The Proud Tower: A Portrait of the World Before the War, 1890–1914.* New York: Ballantine Books, 1962.

U.S. Holocaust Memorial Museum. "Dachau." Jewish Virtual Library. www.jewishvirtuallibrary.org/jsource/Holocaust/dachau.

INDEX

ABOUT THE AUTHOR

Marvin B. Durning, born and raised in New Orleans, is the son of a U.S. Marine Corps officer. He graduated from Dartmouth College, received a master's degree after two years at Oxford University on a Rhodes Scholarship, and graduated from Yale Law School. He served as a naval officer during the tense years of the Korean War and the Cold War struggle over Germany's future. After service in the Office of Naval Intelligence and aboard a destroyer, he was assigned to naval intelligence in Germany. Returning to civilian life, he became an educator and a lawyer. Durning is also an early leader in the environmental movement and was appointed by President Jimmy Carter as assistant administrator for enforcement in the U.S. Environmental Protection Agency. He and his wife Jean live in Seattle.